KU-033-091

Stephanides Brothers'

GREEK MYTHOLOGY

THE ODYSSEY

൭

Retold by Menelaos Stephanides
Drawings by Yannis Stephanides

Translation
Bruce Walter

SIGMA

THE ODYSSEY

Made and published in Greece
ISBN: 960-425-062-0
© 1997 Sigma Publications
Second run 1999

20, Mavromihali Street, Tel.3607667, Fax.3638941
GR-106 80 ATHENS

AN ORACLE FORETOLD that Troy would never be taken without Achilles; another said that Heracles' arrows would be needed, too; a third, that Neoptolemus had to join the fight; and a fourth, that the Achaeans must lay their hands on the Palladium. No oracle claimed Troy would not fall without Odysseus. Yet Priam's city would never have been conquered without the intelligence, persistence and valour of this hero; for it was he who conceived the Wooden Horse in which the Greeks entered Troy. Nor was this all. Odysseus was the one who found Achilles when his mother had hidden him away. It was he who brought Heracles' arrows ftom Lemnos; who brought Neoptolemus to Troy; and last of all, it was Odysseus who contrived to steal the Palladium from the Trojans! Although no prophesy may have foretold it, Troy would never have fallen without Odysseus. Ten years it took for towered Ilium to fall. Almost another ten had passed since then, and only he had still not found his way back home. No man knew whether he was alive or dead. Yet the gods knew: Odysseus was alive and would return.

TABLE OF CONTENTS

ODYSSEUS IS ALIVE AND WILL RETURN

Muse, goddess, help me to set down in song the travails of resourceful Odysseus, lashed by the waves so many years since he set foot upon the sacred walls of Troy, always longing to return home with his comrades. Yet those comrades perished to a man in punishment for slaughtering the oxen of Helios, the sun-god.

Sooner or later, all the other Achaeans who had not been killed in the war or on the stormy seas were to make their way back home, while the man who yearned for his house and his dear wife more deeply than them all had still not returned. He was held prisoner in a cave by the radiant goddess Calypso, who wanted him for her husband. Even when, with the passing of the years, the longed-for time to begin the voyage back arrived, struggles awaited him in his own palace. For though the other gods were united in their sympathy, Poseidon held out a bitter grudge against him, and would not let him reach his beloved island, Ithaca. At this moment, however, the sea-god happened to be far away in Ethiopia, whose people were offering up rich sacrifices to him; and while he rejoiced in this, the rest of the immortals met on Olympus. Zeus was the first to speak. He had been thinking of Aegisthus, and how Orestes had won great glory killing him.

"What fools men are," he said, "to blame their miseries on us immortals when it is their own rash deeds that bring them down and not their destiny. Take Aegisthus, for example: while Agamemnon was away at war, he stole his wife and throne; and when the king returned he murdered him in his own palace. We sent Hermes to warn him not to do it, and to return Queen Clytemnestra to her husband. Yet did he listen while our messenger was advising him for his own good? No! – and now he has paid the price in full."

Then Athena spoke:

"Aegisthus got the punishment he deserved. May all who sink to such dishonour suffer likewise. What tears my heart is the thought of clever, brave Odysseus, languishing years now, far from his own people, a prisoner on an island in the middle of the boundless sea. Atlas' daughter, Calypso, has kept him there for almost a decade, trying with fair, false words to wipe all recollection of his homeland from his memory, while all the poor fellow longs for is to see a little distant hearth-smoke rising from the hills of Ithaca before he dies. Why does your heart not ache for him, Olympian? Could it be you are not satisfied with the sacrifices he has offered to you, and that is why you are so angry with him?"

"My child, how can you let such words escape you?" Zeus replied. "Can I forget that splendid fellow Odysseus, with his matchless strength and wisdom, and the rich sacrifices he has offered all the gods? The seas, however, are ruled by Poseidon, the earth-shaker, who has borne him unrelenting hatred ever since he put out the eye of his son, the Cyclops Polyphemus. This is why he keeps him far from home and weighs him down with endless bitter troubles. Yet now the time has come for other gods to help Odysseus get back to his homeland. The earth-shaker cannot bear his grudge for ever, against our wills."

Athena rejoiced to hear his words.

"Lord Zeus," she said, "since we have decided it is time for Odysseus to return, let us despatch winged Hermes to the island of Ogygia to tell the goddess Calypso of our resolve. I myself will go to seek his son Telemachus, to put heart into him and show him how to stand up to those hateful suitors who are competing for his mother's hand in marriage and eating the palace cellars bare while they are waiting. I shall tell him, too, to go to Pylos and to Sparta for news of his father's home-coming."

Zeus and all the other gods agreed, whereupon Athena took up her heavy war-lance and sped through the air like lightning, from Olympus to Ithaca. When she arrived, she took the form of Mentes, king of Taphos, and walked up to the threshold of the palace. In the courtyard sat the suitors, whiling away their time in games of dice. Their orderlies and servants were busy preparing them a meal; some sponging down the tables, others cutting up the meat, while others still were watering the heavy wine and pouring it into goblets.

Telemachus was the first to spot the stranger. At that moment he had been thinking of his father, and as he sat there, his ears buzzing with the suitors' noisy chatter, he said to himself, "Ah, if only he would suddenly appear and throw them out, and take the reins of power back into his hands!" As these thoughts passed through his mind, his eyes fell on the newcomer and he rose and went across to him, for it seemed ill-mannered to leave a visitor standing there alone. On reaching him, he grasped his hand in friendship and relieved him of the heavy spear he carried.

"Welcome, stranger," said Telemachus. "Please come in and make yourself at home. Sit down, eat, then tell us who you are and what has brought you here."

With these words, he led the man who was really Athena into the lofty palace. On entering, he set her weapon in a fine, carved spear-rack, where others belonging to Odysseus stood. Then he seated the goddess on a lovely, decorated throne, spread with fine linen and with a footstool at its base. Taking another carved chair for himself, he sat down next to her, well apart from the suitors, so that his visitor would not be bothered by their noise while he tried to learn news of his father. A serving-girl immediately brought water and poured it over their hands as they washed them in a silver basin. Then she brought a polished table for them, which the steward set with one tasty dish after another, while an attentive orderly stood at their side to keep their plates and wine-cups filled.

By now the suitors' tables had been set as well, and they attacked their meal with vigour, downing one overflowing cup after the other. When they had eaten and drunk their fill, their fancies turned to dance and song. A harp was brought and put into the hands of Phemius, the sweet-voiced singer, who, through no wish of his own, the suitors had appointed as their entertainer. He brushed his fingertips against its strings, and as he began to play, Telemachus bent low to his unknown visitor, so that the others might not hear.

"Kind sir, I hope you will not think me rude if I say something to you, but you can see that all these fellows care about is having a good time. Their host's bones may be rotting — who knows where? — and yet they are quite happy to eat and drink at his expense. If only he were suddenly to appear before them here, they'd gladly give all the treasure in the world for a quick pair of heels! He is dead and gone, though, and we have no hope of ever seeing him again, whatever some may say about him coming back. But now, stranger, tell me who you are, what family and country you come from, what brings you to our island, and what you want of us. Tell me, is this your first trip to Ithaca, or are you an old friend of our royal house? For I know my father was always fond of good and worthy men."

Athena had a ready answer to his questions.

"My name is Mentes," she replied. "I am the son of the renowned Anchialus and I rule over a nation of sea-going folk, the Taphians. I am on my way to Cyprus, to take on a cargo of copper, and since my voyage brings me to your parts I decided to put in for a brief call. Your father and I have long been friends, and should you visit your grandfather, the old warrior Laertes, do not forget to ask him about me. I know he does not come down to the city any more, but ekes out a miserable existence on the mountainside. They say that the only person he has left to take care of him is an old serving-woman who gives him something to eat and drink when his poor old knees give out from working on the steep slopes of his vineyard. Anyway, the reason that I called is because someone told me his son Odysseus had returned. However, it seems that the gods are still placing obstacles in his way. He is alive, but on some

...Yet let me ask you, if I may: Who are all these fellows?...

distant island encircled by the waves, held prisoner by evil men. Yet I'll tell you one thing, though I am no seer and cannot read the signs: even if they are keeping him in chains, he'll find a way of making his escape, and the day of his return is not far off. It is not often that one meets a man of his cunning and resource. But tell me, are you really his son? Such a splendid, tall young man already! Your face is very much like his, and you have his eyes and manner."

"Yes," sighed Telemachus, "such has been my fortune: to have for a father the unluckiest man the world has ever known."

"But with a fine son, all the same," Athena told him gently. "The gods will not allow a breed as illustrious as this to sink into oblivion! Yet let me ask you, if I may: Who are all these fellows? How can they have the gall to carry on like that? It's enough to make any decent man see red!"

"Since you are a friend, I will tell you all our woes," Telemachus replied. "This would be a happy house, if only my father could be here. Yet he is lost because the gods were envious of his exploits. Ah, even if I knew that he had fallen at Troy, among his comrades, it would be some consolation – for then at least a monument could be raised to him and I revere his memory. As things are, he has disappeared ingloriously and left me with a host of bitter troubles – for it is not only the loss of my father I lament, but all these fortune-hunters you see flocking to our house.

They are the sons of the noblemen of Zacyntus, Cephalo-
nia, Dulichion and Ithaca, all competing for my mother's
hand in marriage. They abuse our hospitality and eat us out
of house and home. They will not budge from here until my
mother chooses one of them. Our fortune is draining away
before our eyes, and on top of that they have made threats
on my life."

Flushed with indignation, Athena answered sharply:

"Telemachus, you are a child no longer, but a full-grown
man. If only Odysseus were here, with his matchless
cunning and bold strength, arriving unannounced to stand
here in the doorway with shield and helmet, carrying two
spears, just as I once remember him! Then you would see
these fellows buckle at the knees as they saw their doom
flash forth from his eyes! However, let me give you some
advice. Call all the people of the island to a meeting; tell
them what you are suffering at these suitors' hands. Then
order these drones to pack their bags and go back where
they came from. Call on the gods as witnesses that they will
come to a sorry end if they do not leave the palace. And
another thing: if you know what's good for you, you'll take
the trouble to find out whether your father is alive or dead.
Take twenty good oarsmen and your fastest ship and go to
Pylos to find old Nestor. If he knows nothing, at least he
will give you good advice. Then make your way to Menelaus, in Sparta. He was the last man to return from Troy,
and surely he will have some news for you. If you hear

your father is alive, be patient and await him; he will return. But if you learn that he is dead, then raise his tomb-mound high and offer funeral sacrifices. When that is done, make sure you get rid of these hangers-on. You're a grown man now, Telemachus, and whether by stealth or direct action you must find a means to do away with all of them. You know what fame Orestes won when he killed Aegisthus, who murdered his illustrious father. You are a tall and fine young fellow, too; so show your strength and daring, that future generations may speak of you with awe. Now the time has come for me to leave. My men await me and I have stayed too long already. Think my words over, and find a way of bringing them to pass."

"Stranger, you have spoken to me like a father," Telemachus replied. "I shall not forget the counsels you have given me. But do not be in such great haste to leave. Stay to have a bath and relax, then go back to your ship refreshed, bearing a present I give with all my heart; something lovely and precious, such as a man gives only to his dearest friends."

"I must leave, Telemachus," Athena answered, "so do not try to keep me longer. As for the gift you want to give me, keep it until the next time that I come, and I will give you one of equal value in return."

With these words, the goddess transformed herself into an eagle and soared into the heavens. Telemachus stared up at her in wonder. He knew now that it was not a king called

Mentes who had spoken with him, but Athena herself, and this filled him with new strength and courage. He would follow to the letter the advice the goddess had given him.

Phemius was still singing, and they were all listening in silence. His song told of the Achaeans' return from Troy. Hearing it from her chamber, Penelope came down the stairs accompanied by two serving girls. Her eyes were filled with tears.

"Phemius, you know many other tales," she told him, "tales which have been set to song to charm the ears of men. Sing one of those to the company, and let them drink in silence. But do not sing this song again, for it makes my heart bleed and tears my breast with pain beyond endurance. As long as I live, I shall never forget my husband, whose fame has spread over the length and breadth of Greece."

"Why blame the singer, mother?" Telemachus answered reasonably. "What fault is it of his? Blame Zeus, who orders all according to his wishes. Besides, was my father the only one who lost his way back home? There were many others who did not return. So go up to your rooms and mind your own concerns. Keep the servants at their work and leave the rest in men's hands, starting with me — for I'm the ruler now in this house!"

Penelope was at a loss for words. Telemachus had never stood up to her like this before. 'He has become a man!' she told herself, a secret joy sweetening her bitter pain, and she gladly submitted to his orders.

When this peerless woman had left them, the suitors became noisy.

"Stop!" roared Telemachus through the hubbub of their conversation. "I will have you here no longer. Tomorrow I will call my people to a meeting and tell them what has been going on between these walls!"

The suitors bit their lips in chagrin, wondering where Telemachus had found the spirit to speak to them so boldly. Antinous, the brashest of them all, got up and said:

"How did you pluck up the courage to talk to us like this? Was it given you by the gods, perhaps? Don't imagine that Zeus will ever let you take the throne, though, even if you are Odysseus' son!"

"Leave the lad alone, Antinous," sneered Eurymachus, another of the would-be bridegrooms and a sly, underhand fellow. "Who shall reign over Ithaca, the gods alone can say. But tell me, child," he said, addressing Telemachus, "who was that you were talking with before? Did he bring some news of your father, or did he come on his own business? He seemed to be a nobleman. How is it that he left without making himself known to us?"

"It's not the throne that troubles me, but my father's disappearance!" Telemachus retorted. "Of all the soothsayers my mother has called in, there's not one that I believe, for I am no longer a child, Eurymachus. As for the stranger, I will tell you: he is an old friend of my father's, from

Taphos. Mentes is his name, and he's the son of the re-nowned Anchialus."

That is what he said, although he knew the stranger had been Athena herself.

Next day, at Telemachus' command, the criers summoned the people to assembly. A large crowd gathered, and they were joined by the suitors. Last of all, Odysseus' peerless son arrived. He was dressed in his finest tunic, a belted sword at his waist and finely-crafted sandals on his feet. There was an aura of heavenly grace about him; and as he advanced to take his seat upon his father's throne, he seemed more god than man.

The first to speak at the assembly was Aegyptius, an old warrior now bent with years. Addressing Telemachus, he said:

"You seem a reasonable young man. May the gods bless you, and Zeus keep you always under protection. Only tell me this: why is the meeting being held? We have not gathered in this place since Odysseus left for Troy. Are our men on their way home, perhaps? I long to see my son, and yet I fear that he is lost for ever." And with these words, he hid his face between his hands, for his eyes had filled with tears.

Then the public crier gave the speaker's staff to Telemachus. Taking it, he rose and said:

"I only wish that I had news to give you of our men. If it

were so, I would have learned about my father, too. But I know nothing. The reason I have called you here is to tell you of two great troubles of my own. The first is that the one man who could have upheld peace and order, and was like a father to us all, is lost. The second, and greatest, is all the suitors who have been living off my mother's hospitality for three years now, although she finds the very sight of them repugnant. They force themselves upon us without a trace of shame, eat up our stores, slaughter our beasts, swill down our choicest wines and blithely ignore the evil they are doing us. The worst of it is that no man of Odysseus' mettle is here to chase them out. Thus I have no choice left but to fight them on my own, come what may. Yes, listen to me, suitors! Fear the gods and leave, lest they turn their wrath upon you. Or did my father tyrannize his people, and am I being punished for his sins? No! My father was a kind and reasonable man, as all of you well know."

At this, he flung the speaker's staff from him disgustedly, and his eyes filled with tears of helpless rage.

All the people pitied him, but not the suitors. Antinous even had the gall to stand and tell him:

"Watch your tongue, young man. It's not we suitors who are to blame, but your mother herself. She has more tricks up her sleeve than any other woman in the land. Why, she even fooled us with some tale about weaving a funeral shroud for old Laertes, saying that as soon as it was finished she would make her choice among us. But did she

"...But did she ever finish? No! For every night she would
unravel her day's work, the sly creature... "

ever finish? No! For every night she would unravel her day's work, the sly creature. She kept us hanging on like fools for three whole years, until we caught her drawing out the threads by lamplight. Now it's your turn to listen. Send your mother to her father, and let him choose, alone or with her help, which one of us he wants. Otherwise, I warn you both that if the only thing she cares about is making us a laughing-stock and winning a reputation for herself at our expense, then we shall stay right where we are, until we have eaten you out of house and home!"

"Listen, Antinous," Telemachus retorted, "my mother gave birth to me and raised me, and I will not turn her out of her own house, whether my father is alive or dead. If you had a single spark of decency left in you, you would leave Odysseus' palace and go to your own homes, each offering hospitality in his turn. But if it does not trouble your consciences to eat your way through another man's fortune, then I shall call upon the gods for help, and mighty Zeus will make you pay for what you've done, you miserable wretches, when he sends Charon here to scythe you down!"

The moment Telemachus had said these words, Zeus sent two eagles, who swept in with their broad wings outstretched and began to circle above the assembled people, in a sure omen of impending catastrophe. Then they launched themselves upon each other, tearing at head and neck with knife-sharp talons. And when at last they left,

...Zeus sent two eagles, who began to circle above
the assembled people, in a sure omen of impending
catastrophe...

they flew off to the east, a certain sign that this had been some message from the gods.

Everyone wondered what was to come, and many were afraid. Then the seer Alitherses, a noble old man who could interpret all the signs in the heavens, came forward and said:

"Listen, all of you – but especially the suitors, for a grim fate awaits them. It will not be long before Odysseus appears. The day of his return to Ithaca draws near, and with it the death and destruction he is preparing for you. So, even at this late hour, put an end to your abuses. That is all I have to say. You all know me. I never prophesy unless I feel the power of the god within me. What I told Odysseus has come to pass: 'You will return home in the twentieth year,' I said, 'unknown, and with all your comrades perished'. Now, all is being fulfilled."

The prophetic words of Alitherses were greeted with insolent scorn by Eurymachus.

"Go and foretell the future somewhere else, old man!" he sneered. "This is a tale for your sons' ears, not for ours. They are the ones whose safety should concern you. I can 'prophesy' as well you. The sky is full of birds, and where they fly is neither here nor there. Yet you would have us believe that Odysseus is returning! He's gone for ever, though, and too bad you didn't croak along with him and spare us all your fraudulent fortune-telling! There is no one now for us to fear, not even Telemachus, for all that he's found his tongue and started threatening us with talk of gods. No, we'll eat the palace clean and serve them right, since his mother wants to make fools of us by always putting off this marriage. Don't let the sweet Penelope think she can discourage us. There's not one of us that does not want her."

"Listen, Eurymachus and you other suitors," Telemachus replied, "I have no intention of going on my knees for mercy. In fact, your words are not worth my attention. It is enough that the gods see all and the people now know everything. All I want is to find a ship to take me to Pylos and then on to Sparta, to learn news of my father. If I hear he is alive, then I will wait for him. If, on the other hand, I am told that he is dead, then I will build a memorial in his name and offer up the fitting funeral sacrifices. After that, I would be free to tell my mother to remarry, if she wished."

Then Odysseus' old steward, Mentor, rose to his feet. He was a wise man and a faithful friend.

"Hear what I have to tell you, men of Ithaca," he said. "We should have had a cold and heartless king, who ruled us with a rod of iron – for that is all we merit. We have forgotten how kind Odysseus was to us, a father to us all, in fact. As for the suitors, if that's the way they want to act, then let them. If our lord should suddenly return, then they shall see how dearly they will pay for everything. But all you others, what are you doing about it? A whole people, and you cannot bring a few proud men to heel?"

Liocritus, another of the suitors, gave this insolent retort:

"Mentor, you're nothing but a loudmouth! Why, we're the cream of the finest families in the land. Do you think your islanders would dare to take us on? Even if Odysseus were to return and find us eating bare his larder, much as he might want to throw us out, he would not even have the time to see his dear Penelope again. No, he'd come to an ugly end in his own house! So stop talking nonsense, and get along with you. Take Alitherses, if you like, and prepare a ship for the voyage Telemachus boasted he would make. You'll be wasting your time, though; the lad would rather sit and wait in Ithaca than risk his neck wandering in unknown parts. That's all I have to say, and now it's time we went our separate ways!"

With these words, the suitors left and the assembly broke up.

Then Telemachus made his way down to the shore, and having washed his hands in the salt sea, he raised them to the heavens and cried:

"Daughter of Zeus, when you came yesterday you gave me hope and courage. Now, help me to accomplish the voyage that you counselled!"

As he spoke, Athena took on the form of Mentor, Odysseus' trusty steward, and appearing at his side she told him:

"You can achieve your goal, Telemachus, for you are a true son of Odysseus. Few sons are like their fathers. Most are worse, and the better ones are rare. But you lack neither the courage nor the good sense of the man whose loins you sprang from, and so I believe that you will carry off your mission successfully. Do not concern yourself about the suitors. Their insolence and malice will bring destruction down on them one day. As for the voyage, you can count upon my aid. I shall find you a swift vessel and a sturdy crew and come with you myself to be your guide. All you need do is go back to the palace and make ready the provisions you must take with you."

Telemachus, of course, did not know it was the goddess who had spoken to him. He was pleased enough to think he would have Mentor's help, and went back home in a lighter frame of mind.

The suitors were already in the courtyard, skinning sheep and goats. When they saw Telemachus, they decided to make fun of him. With an ironic laugh, Antinous approached and grasped him by the hand.

"Telemachus, my proud young cockerel!" he sneered. "Why don't you take a seat with us and join the feast? We'll find a ship for you, my lad, and give you the finest sailors on the island, too, so you can search for your dear father."

"Enough of that, Antinous!" Telemachus retorted. "Do you imagine I would join your drunken revels? I've had as much of you as I can tolerate. Just let me find a way, and you shall see!" And with this, he snatched his hand away.

Seeing his anger, another of the young bullies turned jeeringly to his fellow-suitors:

"Don't let Telemachus upset you. He's a good lad, really. A pity that he's leaving, though. I'm afraid he will wander off and get himself lost, just like Odysseus, and then we'll have the trouble of dividing all his worldly goods amongst us! We won't share out the palace, though. That will go to the one who takes his mother."

However, Telemachus had more important things to do than pay attention to their teasing. Leaving them to their witty remarks, he went off to find Eurycleia, his good old nurse-maid. When he was little, she had brought him up like her own child, watching over him by night and day with tender care as he grew into a man. Laertes had taken her from her father while still a girl, in exchange for twenty oxen. She was such a good soul that he loved and honoured her as highly as his own wife, Anticleia, although he never took her to his bed, for fear of arousing his wife's wrath.

Telemachus went down to the cellar with his nurse. He set aside all the provisions that were needed, Eurycleia filled twelve jars with wine, and everything was then piled in a corner.

"I will come for them tonight," Telemachus said. "I am going on a voyage to Pylos, then to Sparta. I want to learn news of my father."

Eurycleia trembled at his words.

"What has got into you, my child?" she wailed and burst

out crying. "Do not leave, my son, or you, too, will be lost in foreign parts. The moment that they see you've gone, the only thing those suitors will be thinking of is how to stop you getting back again, so they can share your fortune out among themselves. They'll be lying in wait for you, the villains, and the moment you return, they'll do away with you. Stay here, Telemachus. There's no need to go running off into the unknown."

But Telemachus was not Odysseus' son for nothing. He knew what must be done.

"Cheer up, nanny," he reassured her. "I would not set off on a voyage like this unless I had the backing of some god. All I ask is that you swear no word of this reaches my mother's ears until twelve days have passed. I do not want her to learn that I have gone, and spoil her lovely face with crying."

Eurycleia had no choice but to give her solemn word.

Meanwhile Athena, this time taking Telemachus' shape, had gone to choose a ship. Its owner was Noemon, an old friend of Odysseus. She also picked out twenty seamen, all faithful to Telemachus. Wasting no time, they began to get the vessel ready for its voyage. Next the goddess went swiftly to the palace, where she contrived to make the suitors drink even more than usual. It was not long before they were so fuddled that the winecups were slipping from their fumbling hands, and they all staggered off to bed in their houses in the city. When this was done, Athena took on Mentor's form once more and came to find Telemachus.

"I have made all the preparations for the voyage," she told him. The ship is waiting in the harbour, with the sailors at the oars. We must leave immediately. There is no time to be lost."

Without delay, they made their way down to the shore. The vessel lay there, swift and lovely, and Telemachus gazed at it admiringly.

"Comrades," he called out to the bronzed young seamen, "come and help me load up with provisions. Everything must be done in secret. Nobody knows that we are leaving except my faithful old nurse-maid."

In the darkness of the night, they carried all the food and wine on board, then set off on their voyage. Mentor, who was of course none other than Athena herself, sat in the stern with Telemachus standing at her side. Driven forward by the goddess, the fleet ship cut cleanly through the waves, and by morning they had already reached the coast of Pylos.

As they sailed in, a splendid sacrifice was being offered to Poseidon on the shore. The men of Pylos were present in great numbers, divided into nine groups of five hundred, and each group was sacrificing nine oxen to the god. Old Nestor was there, too, together with his sons.

Telemachus and Mentor came ashore and walked across the sand to meet them. Being young and inexperienced,

Odysseus' son was hesitant. "How can I face wise Nestor, and put questions to a king who has ruled over three generations of men?" he asked himself. However, Athena gave him the spirit that he needed.

"Go on," she told him. "He's a good, straightforward man and will hear you out with patience. Beg him to tell you all he knows, and he will not answer you with lies."

As they moved forward, Mentor, took the lead. When they drew near the dais where the old king and his sons were sitting, Peisistratus, his youngest boy, stood up and hastened to greet them. Reaching their side, he extended a welcoming handshake and led them to the table that stood near his father. Cutting two portions of ox-liver, he handed them to the guests, then filled a golden cup with wine, which he passed to Mentor first.

"Pray to Poseidon, stranger," he commanded, "for you have chanced to come at the very moment we are sacrificing to him. When you have done honour to the god and drunk your fill, pass on the cup to your companion, that he may do him honour, too. He is the younger – no more than my age, perhaps – and so I give the cup to you in precedence."

Athena was pleased by the respect the young prince showed her in her human guise, and so she offered up prayers to Poseidon and begged him to grant health and happiness to Nestor, his sons and all the men of Pylos. When she had finished, she gave the cup to Telemachus, so he could shake out the last drops and make his wishes, too. Meanwhile, the sacrificial meat had been drawn off the spits, and carefully shared out to all, so that none had less than the portion which was fitting to his rank. When everyone had eaten his fill, old Nestor rose and said:

"Now the time has come when I may be allowed to put some questions to my guests. Who are you, sirs, and why have you come here, over the wide seas?"

Telemachus answered the old man's question with all the confidence Athena had put into his heart.

"Honoured Nestor, son of renowned Peleus," he addressed him, "I am Odysseus' son, and I have come from Ithaca to ask what you can tell me of my father, the man who breached the lofty walls of Troy. You fought with him, and may know something. We know where and how the others who did not return were killed. He is the only one of whom we can learn nothing – and I beg of you, on bended knee, to reveal what you know. Say, is he dead, or perhaps still alive somewhere, but suffering and unhappy? I beg you, do not conceal the truth from me out of pity, but, if you know it, give it to me as it stands, however black."

"Ah, such memories you bring back to me, my boy!" the noble old warrior sighed. "What an ordeal we went through to capture Priam's city, and how much more we endured before we reached our homes again. Those of us who did, that is, for there were all too many who never made it back.

How can I tell you all that happened? Were I to do so, my
tale would last for days, and you would tire of it and leave
before I was half finished. So, it's Odysseus' son who
stands before me! How wonderfully you spoke out, lad.
Just like your father: charming and persuasive. We never
exchanged a bitter word, we two, for all we ever wanted
was the Achaeans' good. But, alas, Zeus scattered our ships
when we set sail for home, and I have never seen him since.
Not that I have any reason to complain of my own luck. It
was not long before I was back in Pylos, safe and sound.
Most of our people had a rough voyage of it, though. Some
were lost and others were blown here and there upon the
waves for years."

Continuing his story, the noble old man told of the adventures of Menelaus and Helen, who roamed the seas for
eight long winters until they finally reached Sparta. He
spoke of Agamemnon, too, who met a hideous death at the
hands of the treacherous Aegisthus the moment he set foot
in Mycenae. Name after name dropped from his lips, but he
knew nothing of Odysseus.

"Go to Sparta, though," he said at last. "Menelaus may
know something, for he was the last of us to return. Take
the ship that brought you, or beach it here, if you prefer,
and I will give you a chariot and horses, to get there over-
land. It's safer, and I can spare one of my sons to guide you
on your way."

"I agree, my lord," Athena answered. "Now it is time to

sleep, though, and we must be back on board."

"Sleep on the ship?" protested Nestor. "I am not so poor I cannot offer you a good, soft bed and fine-spun blankets. How could I leave my dear friend's son to spend the night on a hard deck?"

"You are right," Athena said once more. "Telemachus must not decline your offer. I shall stay aboard, however. I need to tell the crew our plans, and tomorrow I must pay a visit to your neighbours the Cauconians, on some business of my own. Just send Telemachus to Sparta, as you said, and give him one of your sons to guide him there."

When Athena had spoken, she suddenly transformed herself again, and from being Mentor, she suddenly became an eagle and soared into the heavens.

Amazed at what his eyes had seen, old Nestor grasped Telemachus by the hand and said:

"My friend, you will not prove to be a weak man or a coward, if you already have the gods to aid you. My wits did not deceive me. That was Pallas Athena herself who stood there at your side!"

Next morning, at first light, Nestor's sons made ready a sturdy chariot and harnessed their swiftest horses to the shafts. Young Peisistratus offered his services as guide. The old king came to wish them a safe journey and expressed his hope that they would come back with good news.

It took Peisistratus and Telemachus two days to reach

Sparta. When they arrived, they drew up before the palace gates. Seeing them, one of Menelaus' trusted comrades ran to give him warning.

"Noble Menelaus," he gasped, "two strangers have arrived, young lords so fair they might have Zeus' blood in their veins. They are in a splendid chariot, outside the palace gates. What is your command? Should they dismount here, or shall I send them elsewhere to be entertained?"

"Don't ask such foolish questions!" Menelaus retorted angrily. "Have you forgotten how often strangers gave us food and shelter, when our need drove us to knock at unknown doors in foreign lands? Now that we can offer hospitality ourselves, how can we possibly tell those whom Zeus sends us to go and sleep elsewhere? So hurry up and get those horses from the shafts and bring these young lords to our table!"

Menelaus' command was swiftly obeyed.

When they were led into the stately hall, Telemachus and his companion stood dazzled by its opulence. Not for long, however, for as they were gazing at the gleaming luxury around them, servants arrived and led them to a marble bath-house. When they had scrubbed them well and anointed their bodies with sweet-smelling oil, they dressed them in fine tunics and conducted them to seats beside Menelaus. Immediately, other serving women brought bread and various side dishes. Then the carver brought in meat of every kind, while a steward filled golden cups with wine.

"Welcome," said Menelaus. "Enjoy the food that's set before you, and when you have dined we shall enquire who you noble youths may be – for there is no concealing the fact that you are both high-born."

With these words, he took two choice cuts from the roast which the carver had brought specially for him, and offered them to the strangers.

When the two young men had eaten and drunk their fill, Telemachus leant over and spoke to Peisistratus in a low voice, so that the others would not hear.

"Such wealth!" he whispered. "It makes me dizzy just to look at it. A palace like this could only belong to Zeus."

Yet although he had spoken softly, Menelaus caught his words.

"No, lads," he answered. "There's no mortal on this earth who could have such wealth as mighty Zeus. Perhaps the style I live in could stand comparison with any other man's, but not with his. Besides, however many worldly goods I have, the troubles that I went through getting them were greater still. Eight years I wandered in foreign lands on my voyage home from Troy. Granted, I acquired immense amounts of treasure on the way, from Cyprus, Phoenicia, Egypt, Ethiopia and Libya – but then I had lost a huge fortune of my own before all that. Your fathers must have told you how I was robbed. Many brave men gave up their lives for me at Troy, and I remember them and weep. Yet there is one whom my heart mourns more deeply than all the rest together, one whose memory deprives me of my sleep and takes my appetite away. It is Odysseus that I grieve for, who suffered more than any for my sake. My heart goes out to his sorrowing family, too; to old Laertes, to his wife Penelope, whose sad forebodings have proved all too true, and to his son, Telemachus. When Odysseus left, he was a new-born baby in his mother's arms. Twenty whole years have gone by since, and still there is no sign of his return."

When he heard about his father, Telemachus could not hold his feelings back, and buried his face in his purple robe, so that Menelaus would not see that he was crying. The king was not deceived, however, and it immediately occurred to him that this young man might be Odysseus' son. He was on the point of asking him directly when his wife, the divinely lovely Helen, came down from her chamber. Such were her beauty and her stately bearing, she might have been the goddess Artemis herself. Two serving-women immediately brought forward a carved throne spread with a woollen rug, while a third set down a silver basket filled with fleecy yarn, with a distaff laid across it. Seating herself upon the throne, she placed her feet on the footstool that stood before it, and asked her husband:

"Do you know these noble youths, Menelaus? It seems to me that one of them looks very like Odysseus. Could it be the son he left behind?"

"That's exactly what I was wondering," Menelaus replied. "I noticed that when I spoke of the sufferings Odysseus endured for me, he hid his face so that I should not see his eyes."

"You have both guessed right," Peisistratus then told them. "This is indeed Telemachus, but being still a youth he is afraid to speak out lest he say something that he shouldn't. I am Peisistratus, son of King Nestor. I brought him here from Pylos, on my father's orders, to see if you had any advice to give him — for his life is set about with difficulties now that his father has been away home so long."

Menelaus was deeply moved by what he heard.

"So the son of my best friend has come into my house! If only his father were here before me, too, I would empty a whole city and present it to him, so he might live here with all his people. In this way we should see each other often, and never part until death's shadow fell on us. Yet it seems some god is set against this happening, and has barred the way that would lead his footsteps back."

As he spoke, his eyes began to fill with tears. Helen wept with him, and Telemachus, and even Peisistratus, who thought of another who had not returned: his brother Antilochus, killed beneath the walls of Troy.

Then Helen, her eyes still wet, offered wine to all of them, adding a few drops distilled from a miraculous herb

...I have come to ask if you know anything about my
father...

which she had brought from Egypt. If any drank of this, their eyes would stay dry for a day, even if they had lost a parent, or a child dearly loved.

Once the potion took effect, and their voices were no longer racked with sobs, they began to talk more freely. Helen was the first to speak. She recalled one of Odysseus' great feats, when he had crept undetected into Troy and stolen the Palladium. To avoid being recognized, he had put on a beggar's rags and forced Diomedes to whip him mercilessly until his body was a mass of weals. No one but Helen had realized who it was, and she had not betrayed him to the Trojans. When he returned to his lines, having accomplished his difficult mission and killed many of the enemy, she did not join the women of Troy in weeping over their dead husbands, but soared on wings of joy. For she had long since repented leaving her home, her daughter and her gay, good-hearted husband. Yet it was the gods who were to blame for all that, and above all Aphrodite, who had blinded her with passion to further her own ends.

When Helen had done, it was Menelaus' turn to speak. He told them of the Wooden Horse, how he had been one of the warriors hidden inside its body with Odysseus, and how the latter had saved them when they were in danger of being discovered. When his tale was over, he asked Telemachus what had brought him so far from his home.

"Menelaus, you whom the gods have looked on with such favour, I have come to ask if you know anything about my father. I want the truth from you, however black and bitter it may be, for all my royal inheritance is being stripped from me while he is away. The palace is filled with heartless enemies: the suitors who imagine that my unfortunate mother will consent to marry one of them."

When Menelaus heard this, he was furious.

"Don't those jackals know what lion-heart's bed they are competing for?" he roared. "They'll come to an evil end one of these days, when Odysseus comes back all unexpected, and falls upon them like a raging beast. For Odysseus is alive, I tell you! I learned it from the old soothsayer of the seas, Proteus — and he is never wrong. I'll tell you the whole story, keeping nothing back. But let's begin at the beginning:

When we left Troy, I was punished harshly by the gods, and rightly so, for I had neglected to offer up due sacrifice before we launched the ships. Because of this, they sent strong north winds down on me, which pushed my vessels far off course. Eight years I was buffeted from one distant land to another, until at last I was cast up by the gods upon an island men call Pharos, off the coast of Egypt. Twenty days they kept us there, with not a breath of wind to stir our sails. Our provisions had run out, and my men's spirit nearly gone, when a sea-nymph found me wandering miserably, alone and far from my companions. Her name was Eidothea, and she was a daughter of old Proteus. Seeing my despair, she was moved to help me.

"My father Proteus comes here every day," she told me. "He can see into the future, and is never wrong. If anyone can help you find your way back to your homeland, it is he. However, you will have to use force to find out what you want, for he never gives away his knowledge freely."

"How can a mortal force a god to tell him that which he does not wish to reveal?" I asked her.

"I shall help you," was the nymph's reply. "All you need do is choose three of your strongest seamen and come back here tomorrow at the hour when the sun is directly overhead. I shall lead you to the place where my father always takes his mid-day sleep. He stretches out to rest among the seals of Amphitrite, queen of the sea. Although he never closes his eyes until he has counted every animal, he will not realize that you are there among them, for I shall find a way of concealing your presence from him. The moment you see that he has fallen asleep, then jump on him, all four of you, and hold on tight. In his struggle to escape, he will change himself from one form to another: from man to beast, from beast to writhing serpent, and even into fire and water. Whatever shape he takes, you must not let him go, but grasp him ever tighter until at last he takes on human form again and asks you what it is you want to know. When he does this, release your hold immediately and demand of him which god is angry with you, how you may find your way back to your homeland, and anything else which you might wish to learn."

And with these words she dived into the sea and was lost to sight beneath the waves.

Next day, I chose three strong and trusted comrades and went to the same place. It was not long before Eidothea appeared again, this time carrying four sealskins. She led us near some caves where she scooped out four hollows in the sand. Instructing us to lie down in them, she covered us with the pelts that she had brought, and soon a whole herd of seals arrived and began to lie down all around us. Sure enough, at noon, old Proteus came. Before lying down to take his rest, he counted all the seals, and us along with them, without suspecting for a moment that we had set a trap for him. When he had dropped off to sleep, we quietly rose and flung our strong arms tight around him. In his efforts to evade our clutches, he transformed himself into a lion, and then a snake, and after that a leopard and a wild boar, and finally into running water and a tall tree in full leaf. But we held on grimly, squeezing with all the strength we had, until at last, exhausted by the struggle, he changed back into his former shape and put this question to me:

"Which of the immortals helped you catch me, son of Atreus? No matter, tell me what you wish to know, then set me free again."

"Why ask who helped us, when you know already?" I answered boldly. "Just tell me which god holds me captive on this island, and how I can get back to my homeland."

"Before your men embarked on the voyage home from

Troy, you should have offered sacrifices to Zeus and the other gods of Olympus. Now you must voyage down to Egypt, to the banks of the River Nile, and make the sacrifices there which you still owe. Only then will the immortals take any pity on you."

"I shall do all that you command," I answered him. "Only tell me one thing more, I beg you: have all our comrades got home safe from Troy – or are there some who'll never see the light of day again?"

"Of all the Achaean leaders," he replied, "only two were lost on the return voyage. Those who died in battle, you know about already. There is a third who is still storm-tossed on the high seas. The first to lose his life on the way home was Ajax, son of Oileus. Poseidon cast him on the rocky shore of Euboea to satisfy Athena, who had good cause to hate him. Even then he could have saved his skin had he but shown respect for the immortals instead of boasting that he would survive the shipwreck in defiance of their will. Poseidon heard him and with his trident struck the rock he clung to. The stone was split in two, one half remaining in its place, the other tumbling down into the foaming sea along with Ajax. And so he perished, swallowing his impious words with a lungful of salt water. Now I shall tell you of the other who was lost, your brother Agamemnon. He, too, came close to perishing upon the craggy coast of Euboea, but was saved by Hera. And when at last he set foot on his native shore, he kissed the land he loved, watering the earth with his hot tears. By this time, however, Mycenae had come under the sway of Aegisthus, who had taken Agamemnon's faithless wife. The moment word came that the king was back, the traitor laid a secret plan to do away with him. Aided by Clytemnestra, he set out a royal banquet and pretended to receive him with great honours. Then, suddenly, Aegisthus threw himself on Agamemnon with a knife and felled him like an ox led to the slaughter."

Knowing the old man's words were always true, I fell to my knees upon the sand and wept for my lost brother, covering my face with my hands to hide it from the sun.

"Do not cry, Menelaus," Proteus told me gently. "Nothing will come of tears; but lose no time in trying to make your way back to your native land – although I do not know whether you will reach it in time to find Aegisthus still alive, or whether Agamemnon's son Orestes will have already cut him down."

In spite of all my grief, my heart was lightened when I heard the old man's final words, and I found the courage to go on with my questions.

"You have told me all you know of these two who are lost," I said, "but I want to know about the third, as well. Who is he, I beg of you. Is he still storm-tossed on the seas, or has he perished like the others? I wish to hear, even if it costs me further bitter tears."

"The third is Odysseus, son of Laertes and king of Ithaca," the old seer replied. "I saw him with my own eyes, weeping and imprisoned on the island of the nymph Calypso. Although he longs to see his home again, she will not let him leave her side. Besides, the unlucky fellow has neither ship nor sailors to carry him away across the water."

That is what the old man of the deep had to tell me of your father, and then he plunged into the sea and disappeared beneath the waves. Then I ordered my comrades to make ready the ships, and in the morning we rowed out from our anchorage and headed for the Nile, where we made the sacrifice we had owed the gods so long. As soon as we were back on board, their anger faded and a steady wind carried us back to the homeland we all longed for. Such were my adventures. But now, Telemachus, stay in my house for ten days or so and let me treat you as an honoured guest deserves. I have precious gifts for you, too: a splendid chariot with three swift horses, and a chalice with which to pour out your libations to the gods, so that you will remember me for all the days of your life."

"Do not keep me here so long, my lord," Telemachus replied. "It is true your stories are so fascinating that I could sit here with you for a year and quite forget my people and my home. But my crew await me down in Pylos, and I have been away too long. As for your presents, I shall cherish them. I shall not deprive you of your wonderful horses, though. Where I come from, there are no

...“I saw him with my own eyes, weeping and imprisoned
on the island of the nymph Calypso.” said Proteus...

plains or meadows for them to graze in, nor open roads for them to gallop on. Mine is a rocky country, though more beautiful than the flat lands which breed horses. That is how all the islands are – and Ithaca more than most."

Menelaus was pleased by what he said and grasped him by the hand.

"You are a true son of Odysseus, and that is why you speak so wisely. I have present to give you in their place, however, a bowl with solid gold around the lip, the work of Hephaestus and a marvel to behold. The king of Sidon gave it to me when I was his guest – and now it shall be yours!"

Meanwhile, on Ithaca, in the courtyard of Odysseus' lofty palace, the proud suitors were whiling away their time with athletics contests. Antinous had won the discus competition, while Eurymachus had come first in the javelin event. Just then, however, Noemon the sea-captain arrived.

"Eurymachus, do you happen to know when Telemachus will be back? He took my ship, but now I have to sail to Elis and need it for myself."

Noemon's words were met with angry consternation, for none of them had believed that Telemachus would actually sail off. They had imagined he was still somewhere around, perhaps out tending his fields.

Antinous jumped to his feet.

"Out with it, now! When did he leave, and who went with him?" he demanded. "And tell me another thing: did he just commandeer the ship from you, or ask it as a favour?"

"He asked me for it and I let him have it. What else can one do when a king's son makes his wishes known? The finest young men on the island went off with him, too. As for their pilot, he looked like Mentor, but must have been some god. For how could I have seen Mentor here in town just yesterday, when I saw him sail off with the others?"

Noemon then left, but his words had filled the suitors with such alarm that they forgot all about their games. Beside himself with rage, Antinous burst out:

"Do you see what Telemachus is up to now? Here we were, thinking he didn't have it in him, and while we sat, this beardless boy has slipped neatly through our fingers and is plotting who knows what against us! Never fear, though, he will not have time to do us harm. With Zeus' aid, we shall finish him off once and for all. Come, ready a fast ship, and twenty of us, with me as leader, will sail off and lie in ambush for him in the straits of Same. He'll pay for this foolhardiness with his life!"

They all fell in with Antinous' plan — but were overheard by Medon, Odysseus' faithful herald, who ran to tell Penelope. He knocked, but before he could speak the queen appeared in the doorway and cried out:

"Herald, who sent you here? Have you come to order the servant-girls to prepare a table for those wicked men? If only the gods might make that meal their last! All day they sit here, devouring the birth-right of my Telemachus, as if their fathers had never told them who Odysseus was! Odysseus, who never harmed a man unjustly, who never had an evil word for anyone, who never carried on like other kings, who show their love to some but vent their hatred on others. But as for these men, you can tell their black souls from their deeds. They have no sense of what they owe their greatest benefactor, the ungrateful wretches!"

"I wish it were no worse, my lady," Medon replied respectfully, "but now they are plotting something twice as bad. They plan to kill Telemachus, who has sailed off to the mainland, to learn news of his father."

When Penelope heard this, her knees gave way and her poor heart nearly burst with grief. For a long time she could not utter a word, and when she finally recovered her powers of speech, she wailed:

"Crier, why did he leave? What drove my son to risk his life upon the foaming seas? Does he want the royal house to die out with no heir?"

"I cannot tell you, madam," Medon answered. "Perhaps he was acting on the instructions of some god, or there again, perhaps it was his own decision. He's no fool, your Telemachus."

Wounded to the heart, Penelope roughly brushed aside the chair which her serving-girls had brought her and sank in tears against the doorpost.

"Why didn't one of you come to wake me up," she sobbed at last, "and warn me that my son was leaving? Perhaps I would have had time to stop him then. Don't tell me not a single one of you knew anything!"

Then old Eurycleia spoke up:

"Take a knife and slaughter me, my lady, or spare my life if you will. I knew, but did not tell you. I gave him food and wine, though I begged him not to go. He made me swear a dreadful oath that I would not breathe a word of it to you until twelve days had passed – for he did not want you crying and spoiling your sweet face."

Then Penelope called on Athena for aid. "Mighty goddess," she cried out, "in the name of all the fatted sheep and oxen that Odysseus ever sacrificed upon your holy altars, I beg you, save my child and free us from these harsh and evil suitors."

Athena listened to her plea, but Penelope's tormentors, who had already set their plan in motion, went by night to a deserted islet with two anchorages, which lay between Same and Ithaca. There they concealed themselves and lay in wait for Odysseus' son.

That same night, the goddess Athena, who felt deep pity for Penelope, sent her sister Iphthime to her in her sleep.

"Do not grieve so, Penelope," said Iphthime's shade. "The gods love your son, and he will come back safely."

"Sister dear," Penelope replied, "how have you come to me from so far away, and how can you tell me to put aside this grief which is driving me out of my wits? First I lose my husband, the finest Achaean of them all, and now my son, rash and inexperienced, has gone headlong into danger. Enemies are waiting to kill him as soon as he returns. How can I not weep at my misfortune; how can my heart not break with pain?"

"Fear not, sister!" the dim form of Iphthime told her, "Telemachus has Athena for his guide and counsellor – and her strength is undefeatable. It was she herself who sent me here to comfort you with these words."

At this the shadow faded and slipped through the doorway into the dark night outside. Penelope slept on, but when she woke her heart was lightened by the memory of the dream-form sent her by the goddess.

THE ADVENTURES OF ODYSSEUS

On Calypso's island

On the orders of almighty Zeus, Hermes winged his way to the island of Ogygia to deliver the gods' verdict to the nymph Calypso: Odysseus must be allowed to find his way back home.

When his plumed feet touched down on the island, he saw before him the great cave where the goddess lived. A fire was burning in the hearth, and a sweet fragrance spread upwards from the resiny logs which smouldered there. So lovely was the glade around the cave, with its cool shade-trees, its brightly-coloured birds and the waters which gushed and gurgled here and there among the rocks, that Hermes stood silent for a long moment, entranced by what he saw.

When he went into the cave, he saw the goddess seated at her loom, singing sweetly as she wove. But Odysseus was not there. He was on the seashore, weeping as he stared out to the horizon and longing, as always, for the hour of his departure.

The moment Calypso set eyes on Hermes she knew him for who he was; for the immortals always recognize each other, although they may live very far apart.

"What brings you to these distant shores, dear Hermes?" she greeted him. "Tell me what you want, and I promise you it shall be done if it lies within my power. But come in first and let me offer you something to refresh you."

Even as she spoke she had set a table with ambrosia and crimson nectar. And when Hermes had licked the last delicious fragrance from his lips, he turned and addressed the lovely nymph.

"You asked me, goddess, what had brought me here from so far away. Zeus sent me, and I had to come, though I had little wish to cross the boundless sea. There's no feasting for a god in those empty wastes of water, no fragrant sacrificial odours wafting through the air. Anyway, the reason I am here is because you have a mortal with you, the unluckiest of men, one who conquered Troy but lost all his companions at sea and was cast up alone upon this island, driven by the wind and waves. Zeus now wishes him to leave. He says it is not written for Odysseus to remain with you for ever, but to see his dear homeland and his people once again."

Calypso was far from pleased by what she heard.

"You gods who live on Olympus are a hard-hearted crew!" she answered bitterly. "You are seized by jealousy whenever you see one of us lesser gods in love with a mortal. That's why proud Artemis killed Orion with an arrow – because Eos, the rosy-fingered dawn, had fallen for his charms. Zeus' thunderbolt struck Iasion down in the flower of his youth for the same reason, just because curly-braided Demeter had taken a fancy to him. That's why you cannot bear for me to have a man as my companion now. Yet do not forget that it was I who saved him from the foaming sea, when he was clinging to a broken keel, lashed by the waves. It was I who gave him food and cared for him. And it is I who shield him from Poseidon's wrath. Just when I was hoping to transform him into an immortal, you come along and tell me I must let him go! Well, let him go then, since none of us can defy the will of Zeus. Yet how will he make the voyage, when he doesn't even have a set of oars to his name, let alone a ship and a crew to man it? Ah well, what must be must be. I shall help him once again, and tell him how to reach the home he yearns for."

"Do as you have promised, Calypso, and without delay – for otherwise Zeus may be angered, and then things will go

badly with you." And with these words Hermes soared off
on his homeward flight, while she made her way sorrowfully down to the shore in search of Odysseus.

She saw him sitting on a boulder, sobbing as he gazed
out over the blue void of the sea. Coming to his side, she
told him:

"Weep no more, Odysseus, for the time has come for
you to go back to your loved ones. Go, take an axe and cut
down some sturdy trees to make a raft. Build the sides high
to protect you from the waves, and launch yourself upon
the sea in it. I shall bring you bread, fresh water and red
wine, so you will not be assailed by thirst and hunger on
your voyage. I shall give you clothes to protect you from
the cold, and loose a gentle breeze which will carry you
swiftly and safely to your homeland, provided that is the
wish of other, higher gods than me."

Odysseus' blood froze in his veins.

"I do not believe you!" he cried out. "Who knows what
harm you plot to do me, lady, telling me to knock a raft
together and risk my life on seas feared by the stoutest
ships! No, I will not do it, unless you swear by the most
binding of all oaths that you are not planning some evil for
me worse than that I now endure."

"Crafty boy," Calypso answered him affectionately,
"what could have put an idea like that into your head? Very
well, I swear – and let my witnesses be the earth and the
high heavens and the waters of the sacred Styx – that my

oath is the most solemn an immortal could give. I wish you nothing but the best, Odysseus. I do not have a heart of stone, but a soft and tender one which feels for you."

With these words, she turned and made her way back to her home in the great cave, and Odysseus followed her. When they arrived, she sat him at the table and placed before him all that he could wish to eat and drink. She seated herself opposite, while her serving-maidens brought ambrosia and nectar. And when they had eaten and drunk their fill, the lovely nymph Calypso began to pour out her complaints.

"Odysseus, do you yearn so desperately to see your home and child again, then? Not that I hold it against you, of course – and may the gods be with you. Yet if you knew the dangers and hardships that still lie before you, you would prefer to stay right here for ever, however much you long to see the wife you miss so much. Don't tell me, though, that I'm inferior to her in looks. It doesn't do for mortal women to rival goddesses in beauty or in grace."

"Believe me, adored goddess," Odysseus replied, "I know Penelope, for all her loveliness, would seem a poor, plain thing in front of you. She is only a woman, after all, while age and care can never mar your divine looks. I would never dream of making any comparison between you. As for the hardships that you warn me of, I can only say one thing: let them come. I am so anxious for the day of my return to dawn, that were the waves to fall on me like mountains once again, I would give battle with them one more time. I have suffered so much already. What is a little suffering more?"

A raft to make the voyage home

In the morning, Calypso gave him a double-headed axe and a well-sharpened adze and led him to a coppice where she showed him tall firs, poplars and other trees whose sap had long run dry and made them suitable for building a good raft.

Odysseus threw himself into the task. He cut down several trees, then trimmed and peeled their trunks. The goddess brought an awl, with which he drilled holes through their breadth and tied them to each other to make a wide, firm raft. To keep the deck dry in high seas, he built stout wooden walls all round. He used another tall, straight tree to make a mast, lashed a cross-beam to it, then fashioned a rudder. From some strong cloth Calypso had brought him he sewed a sail and lashed it to the cross-beam, then rigged the mast and sail firmly in place with good thick cords. When all was ready, he levered the sturdy vessel into the water. It had taken him four days of solid work. On the fifth, the goddess washed him with her own hands and dressed him in sweet-smelling robes. She filled a skin with good red wine, another with water, and in a sack she packed so much food that he would lack for nothing on

...seizing his trident, stirred up the waters till the waves
rose high as mountains...

the voyage home. Last of all, she called down a gentle following wind. Odysseus jumped happily onto the raft and called a farewell to the goddess, whose eyes had filled with tears.

Sitting in the stern, Odysseus clung to the rudder and steered his well-built craft with skill. The island of Ogygia, where Calypso had held him for eight years, soon disappeared over the horizon. Dusk fell, but he did not close his eyes for an instant. All night he travelled by the stars, setting his course by the Pleiades, the Wagoner and the Bear, which never sinks beneath the waves but always revolves in the same spot in the heavens, looking towards Orion.

Poseidon prevents Odysseus' return

Odysseus travelled over the sea for many days like this, always keeping the Bear on his left, as the goddess had advised him; and on the eighteenth morning, the mountain-peaks of a great island loomed out of the sea-mist. It was Scheria, the land of the Phaeacians.

That same day, Poseidon was returning from his visit to the Ethiopians. He was still a long way off, but his sharp eyes spotted Odysseus as he approached the island of the Phaeacians, from where he had been assured an easy voyage home.

"So the gods have changed their minds and let him go!" he exclaimed angrily. "But I'll show him what trouble means, or my name's not Earthshaker!"

With these words, he gathered up a great armful of dark clouds and, seizing his trident, stirred up the waters till the waves rose high as mountains. Pushing the winds before him, he ordered them to blow all at once, from North, South, East and West. The storm that struck Odysseus was terrible beyond belief. He went weak at the knees, and with a deep groan of despair he spoke to his own fearless spirit:

"Alas! The goddess was right to warn me of the trials I would face. Look what clouds Zeus has piled up in the heavens, and what raging winds he's loosed upon me. There is no escaping this. My end has come. Ah, how much luckier were those who fell at Troy, and what ill fortune prevented me from being killed back there, as I fought over dead Achilles, and the enemy's spears fell round me in their thousands! I would be lying now beneath a lofty tomb, in everlasting glory; but instead, fate has decreed I must be lost without a grave, without a single stone to remind men of the spot where the unlucky son of Laertes met his death."

Hardly had this gloomy thought passed through his mind than a great wave loomed above him, smashed down upon the raft with fearful force, tore the rudder from his grasp and plunged him down, down into the depths. The wild wind snapped the mast, caught up the sail and crossbeam and hurled them out across the raging waters, while poor Odysseus, weighed down by his sodden clothes, struggled desperately towards the surface. At last he got his head above the water, coughing mouthfuls of the bitter brine he'd swallowed, then struck out for the raft with all the power in his arms. Thrashing through the water, he got a grip on it and then, for all the lashing fury of the waves which threatened to throw him clear again, he inched himself on board in the very teeth of death. He had just crawled to the middle of the deck when a sea-goddess rose up from the waves. It was Leucothea, who had once been a mortal woman named Ino, a daughter of king Cadmus. The moment she saw the unfortunate Odysseus her heart was wrung with pity for him, and stepping lightly aboard the raft she said:

"Unlucky fellow! Why does Poseidon dash all your hopes so cruelly? Well, let him rage – for there is still a way that you can save yourself. Throw your clothes into the sea and swim with all your strength towards the land of the Phaeacians. If you make the shore, it is ordained you shall find safety there. Just take this veil and tie it to your chest and you need have no fear of drowning. But take it off as soon as you reach land. Throw it back into the sea to me, keeping your face turned away."

As soon as she had given him the magic veil, Leucothea slipped into the sea and was lost to sight beneath the foaming waves.

Odysseus was not convinced, and again a groan escaped him.

"Who knows what trap this goddess may be setting when she tells me to plunge into these wild waters? But I won't be tricked just yet. The shore is far away, and as long as these tree-trunks hold together, I'm staying right where I am. If they do part, well then I'll swim, if that is all that's left to me."

Just then, Poseidon raised a huge wave, mountain-high, and sent it crashing down upon the weakened raft. Like straw blown on the wind, its timbers parted. Odysseus just had time to seize hold of a spar. He straddled it as if he were on horseback, then tore off the clothes which Calypso had given him, and spread the magic veil over his chest, for now he had no choice but to place his trust in Leucothea's advice.

Plunging into the sea, he swam with all his might towards the shore. Again, Poseidon spotted him, but this time he was content to say: "Swim away, then. You've had your share of troubles already. Make for the shore and find some humans to take pity on you – and as for what you've suffered at my hands, well, I hope you're satisfied." And with these words he whipped up his horses and galloped off to his shining palace at Aegae.

Once Poseidon had gone, Athena sped to the battered hero's aid. She immediately restrained the howling winds, leaving only the North wind to push him on towards the land of the Phaeacians. Two days and nights Odysseus struggled through the choppy waters, and a thousand times he looked Charon in the face. But when at dawn on the third day he caught sight of the tree-covered island, his heart was lightened. Summoning his last reserves of strength, he made quickly for the shore; but when he got within hailing distance he saw a line of foam where the waves were breaking on jagged rocks.

"More trouble!" groaned Odysseus. "Those rocks are sharp as knives and the breakers are hitting them with force. There's no beach anywhere, and if the waters throw me on the stones I'm lost. Even if I swim until I reach a flat shore or some inlet the undertow may drag me back again, for I see the Earthshaker's wrath has not yet been appeased."

Just as he was saying this, a towering breaker snatched him up and hurled him down upon the sharp-toothed rocks.

He would have been smashed to pulp upon them had Athena not shown him what to do. Quick as a flash, he got a grip and hung on for dear life; but when the swirling spume sucked back again, it dragged the unlucky Odysseus down to a worse fate: a whirlpool swallowed him and drew him far into the depths. His heroic career might well have ended there, but Athena helped him to reach the surface and swim through the foam until he was well clear of that deadly shore.

On the isle of the Phaeacians

Soon after, riding the crest of a high wave, he caught sight of a river-mouth. "If I can reach there, I am saved," he told himself, and swam towards it with what strength he had left in him. When he was within hailing distance of the inlet, he called out:

"River-god, save me, whoever you are! Save me from Poseidon's wrath and I shall worship you for ever!"

The river heard Odysseus and slowed its tumbling flow. Its waters became smooth as a millpond and our exhausted hero staggered to the shore. His legs gave way and he sank upon his knees with head bowed low, water gushing in torrents from his mouth and nose. Breathless and deprived of speech, he knelt aching in every limb. Finally he managed to gulp in some air and his faltering heart regained its steady beat. Untying the magic veil he had been wearing on his chest, he threw it over his shoulder into the river. The current bore it swiftly downstream into Leucothea's hands, while Odysseus bent and kissed the soil, unable to believe he had been saved. But his heart was heavy in his breast, for he was naked and the chilly night was coming on. Searching around for cover, he found two olive trees upon a knoll. They were growing close together, and their foliage was so thick it would protect him from the keen night air. Burrowing beneath them, he found the ground thick with fallen leaves, and he gratefully scooped out a hollow and stretched out in it, burying his whole body in a leafy blanket. Now he could spend a warm night and not fear the North wind's frozen gusts. And Athena was by his side to close his eyes and pour sweet sleep into his weary limbs.

Once darkness had covered the land and Odysseus was slumbering deeply, Athena went to the palace of the king of the Phaeacians, the renowned Alcinous. There, in a richly-decorated chamber, upon a great carved bed, slept Nausicaa, the king's lovely daughter. The goddess stooped over her pillow and breathed into her mind a dream of her dearest friend, Dymas' daughter, who approached the bed and said:

"Come, Nausicaa, does it do to be so lazy when all your loveliest robes are lying there unwashed, and you may need to wear them? You are old enough for marriage now, and half the young nobles of the island long to have you as their bride, so you must always be beautifully dressed and have fine embroidered gowns ready to give your wedding party. Go now to your father and ask him to have a wagon readied for you, so you can load it with your frocks and sheets and all your other linen, then we shall go down to the river together and wash them."

When Nausicaa woke up in the morning, this dream was still fresh in her memory, and she ran straight to Alcinous.

"Please, father, tell them to hitch a wagon up, so I can take our clothes and wash them in the stream. You must be dressed in fresh, sweet-smelling robes when you meet with the other nobles in council, and my brothers must wear clean clothes when they go to dance. It's my duty to take care of things like this."

Nausicaa was too shy to mention the delightful subject of marriage, but her father realized what she had in mind and ordered a good, stout covered cart to be got ready and two mules harnessed to it. Then Nausicaa brought the clothes and loaded them on board, while her mother handed her food and wine and even a flask of oil for her and the servant-girls to rub themselves with once they had finished all the washing and taken a bathe. Nausicaa climbed up on the cart, seized the reins and whipped up the mules, which set off with her hand-maidens following behind.

When they reached the washing tanks down by the river, the girls unhitched the mules and sent them off to graze, then piled the dirty clothes into the troughs and raced one another to see who could work fastest, till everything was washed and shining clean. Spreading the garments out on the pebbly shore to dry, they ran into the river to bathe, then rubbed themselves down with the oil. Pleased with their day's work, they all sat down to eat, and when their meal was over, they decided to play ball. The weather was as lovely as the girls, but Nausicaa stood out amongst them like Artemis among the wood-nymphs of her train. With a song on her lips, she tossed the ball up in the air and the game began. Time flew by happily, and soon the clothes were dry. Now it was time to gather them and leave, but Odysseus, who had been sleeping nearby since the previous evening, showed no sign of awaking in spite of the girls' shouts and laughter. The exhaustion brought on by so many sleepless nights still kept his eyes shut fast; but Athena did not intend to let him go on sleeping. The next time Nausicaa threw the ball, her hands slipped and it landed in the river. She had thrown it in such a clumsy and amusing way that the others burst out laughing – so loud that it finally woke Odysseus up.

"Where am I?" he asked himself, "in a land of savage, lawless people, or one where folks know right from wrong? I think I heard sweet maidens' voices. Are they water-nymphs, or the daughters of mortal men?" And eager to find out, he emerged from the pile of leaves that he had burrowed into. He was stark naked, though. How could he walk over to where he had heard the girlish voices coming from? Yet just as nothing stops a hungry lion when it spots a plump deer in the distance, so necessity spurred Odysseus on now. Breaking off a leafy branch to hide his nakedness, he made straight for the group of girls.

They were horrified when they caught sight of him. Bloody and salt-caked from his battering at sea, he looked so wild that they scattered in alarm and hid among the trees. But the one who mattered, Nausicaa, the daughter of Alcinous, stood her ground, for Athena herself had given her courage. Odysseus walked up to her. His first thought

...They were horrified when they caught sight of him...

was to throw himself at her feet and clasp her by knees, but in the end he decided just to speak to her, in case his touch offended.

He chose his words with care, speaking gently and persuasively.

"Help me, I beg you, noble maiden, whoever you may be. If you are a goddess, I would liken you to Artemis, Zeus' daughter, so closely do you resemble her in grace and beauty. If you are a mortal, then your parents and your brothers are fortunate indeed. How their hearts must rejoice when they see you leading the dance! More fortunate still the man who takes you for his bride. Forgive me for speaking to you thus, but this is the first time I have seen a maid as fair as you, and I hardly know what I am saying. Only on Delos once were my eyes entranced in such a way, when I saw a young palm tree springing up by Apollo's altar, and its cool beauty left me dazzled and dumbfounded, just as yours does now. I am a man in deep distress, and yet I cannot find the courage to throw myself before you and clasp your knees in supplication. Twenty whole days I have been tossed upon the waves, and yesterday fate cast me on this shore. I have no idea where I may be, and you are the first human being I have seen. I beg you, give me some old cast-off garment to hide my nakedness and point me out which way the city lies. In return for your kindness, may the gods grant you all your heart desires: a husband and a home where two hearts beat as one; for there is nothing in the world that is finer than a loving couple. It is a sight to fill their dear friends with joy, and their enemies with envy."

"Stranger," Nausicaa replied, "it seems to me you are no common wanderer. Yet Zeus allots men joy and suffering as he sees fit, and they must bear their burdens patiently. Now that you have come here, though, we shall not leave you in this state. We shall both give you clothes and lead you to the city, for you have come to the kindly land of the Phaeacians. Our ruler is the renowned Alcinous, and I have the good fortune to be his daughter."

Having said this, she called out to the serving-girls:

"Come over here! Why did you run away? This man means no harm; he's just an unfortunate castaway who needs our help. Zeus sends the poor and unfortunate to us, and what little we can do for them, we always do it gladly. Come, let us help the poor fellow to clean up in the river."

The girls came running up and led him to a sheltered pool, where they gave him clothes and a jar of rubbing oil and told him he could wash.

"First draw aside," Odysseus requested. "I am ashamed to show myself in front of all you lovely maidens."

The girls withdrew and Odysseus began to clean himself, sluicing off the salt that encrusted his broad shoulders and strong arms. He threw water on his face and kneaded his curly hair until it shone again. When his whole body was once more fresh and sweet-smelling, he rubbed it down with oil. Next he put on the clothes that they had left for him. Now he was clean and wearing a fine robe, he was beyond all recognition. For Odysseus had always been a handsome, dashing man, and Athena had given him added grace and stature, so that now, as he came up from the pool and walked across the shore, the girls all stared at him in admiration.

"Zeus had a hand in bringing this man to our island," Nausicaa exclaimed. "When I first set eyes on him, he seemed an ugly fellow but now he seems like a god. If only the man who takes me for his wife could look like him! But come, my girls, give him something to eat and drink."

The maidens quickly brought him food and wine, which he wolfed down, not having put a morsel in his mouth for days.

When his hunger and thirst were satisfied at last, Nausicaa said:

"Now, stranger, let us go up to the city so you can see my father. But keep behind me, hidden among the others; and when the houses come in sight, stay in the forest and come on a little later, on your own. It would not do to have the people see me with you. They are good folk, the Phaeacians, peaceful and hardworking. All they care about is ships and oars and sails, and they have no love for weapons; but there are many idle tongues among them and I do not wish them asking one another, "Who is this splendid man accompanying Nausicaa? Where did she find

him? Do you think she wants him for a husband? Is he a
shipwrecked foreigner, or perhaps some god who has
descended from the heavens to take her for his bride?
Whoever he may be, he's certainly not one of us. So many
Phaeacians have sought her hand, the sons of all our greatest nobles. She has rejected every one of them, and now she
has gone and chosen a stranger." That's the kind of thing
they are capable of saying, and I'll find it mortifying if they
do, for I share their disapproval of girls who make their
choice without having the respect to consult their parents
first, and who go and sleep with a man before they're even
married to him. So just wait awhile where I told you,
stranger, then go up to the city. When you arrive, ask for
my father's house. You'll have no difficulty finding it:
even the children can tell you where it is, and the richest of
the nobles' mansions cannot be mistaken for the palace of
king Alcinous. When you have passed through the courtyard, enter the hall and cross the living-quarters until you
find queen Arete, my mother. You will see her sitting by
the hearth, twisting the fluffy yarn into a ball of wool.
There, too, you will see my father sitting on his throne and
drinking wine. Make straight for the queen, however, and if
you wish to see your loved ones again soon, lay your hands
upon her knees and beg her to come to your assistance. If
she takes pity on you, then you have hopes of seeing the
homeland that you yearn for before long, however many
miles it lies from here."

With these words, Nausicaa climbed into the cart, whipped up the mules and set off for home, accompanied by the stranger and her servants.

When the city came in sight, Odysseus stopped as Nausicaa had told him. And once he was alone, he called on Athena, daughter of Zeus.

"Invincible virgin," he prayed, "you could not hear my voice when Poseidon was intent on drowning me, so hear it now, and grant that the Phaeacians will offer me their sympathy and love."

Athena heard his plea but did not show herself, for she stood in awe of that great god who ruled the seas, and knew with what relentless fury he would pursue Laertes' luckless son.

When sufficient time had passed, Odysseus set off for the city. Once he had passed through the main gate, Athena came to point him out the way. She did not appear before him as a goddess, but took on the form of a girl who appeared to cross his path by chance. When Odysseus caught sight of her, he asked where the palace of king Alcinous lay.

"I am a shipwrecked stranger," he added, "and I seek his help."

"I am going that way myself," the girl replied, "for our house lies nearby. Follow behind me and I will lead the way. Do not speak to anyone you meet along the road, however, for the Phaeacians are a proud people. They have every right to be, of course, being such splendid seafarers. There's not a corner of the world they've not explored in their swift ships which fly like birds, as fast as thought itself."

With these words, she went on ahead and he followed her. Then the goddess wrapped him in a mist so that the Phaeacians could not see him. He saw them all, however, and the city too. He admired the ships and the harbour that they lay in and gazed in wonder at the city squares where the elders stood in conversation. When they reached the dwelling of the king, Athena told him:

"Here is the palace you are looking for. Go in without fear. A bold man soon completes the hardest task, even though he comes from far away. Remember, though, it is the queen whose help you must seek first. Her name is Arete, and she stems from an immortal line, as does Alcinous our king, who cherishes her as no other woman has ever been loved before. Indeed, we all adore her, for she gives aid to all who come to her in need, once she sees they are not evil – and she will help you, too."

Having said this, the goddess left Odysseus and he proceeded boldly on towards the palace. When his eyes beheld its towering walls he stood rooted in amazement. The whole building gleamed in the sunlight, for its ramparts were of bronze, with a band of glittering crystal running round them. Its gates were fashioned of pure gold, as was its roof. At the great portal, two unsleeping guardians stood, a golden and a silver dog made by Hephaestus, who had breathed immortal life into them. Once he had stepped over the threshold, Odysseus was even further dazzled by the wealth and beauty that he found within. Against the walls were beautifully carved thrones for the leaders of the Phaeacians. On graceful pedestals stood golden statues of young men holding lighted torches aloft. Odysseus was feasting his eyes on all of this when his eyes fell on the king and queen, so he hurried over to them. As he approached, the mist that Athena had cast around him faded, and all who were present in the hall stared in surprise at his sudden and miraculous appearance. Taking two steps forward, Odysseus placed his hands upon queen Arete's knees and made his petition to her.

"Mighty queen," he said, "in my sore trouble, I throw myself at your feet, at the feet of your husband, the worthy king of the Phaeacians, and all the proud leaders of your people here assembled, and I beg you to send me on my homeward way – for I have been storm-tossed and separated from my folks this many a year."

Having poured out his woes, he went and sat in the ashes on the hearth. Silence fell, broken at last by old Echeneus, whom all respected for his wisdom. Rising to his feet, he said:

"Alcinous, I do not think it right to let a guest sit in the ashes. If none of us has spoken, it is because we all defer to

...I beg you to send me on my homeward way...

you; but tell him to get up, my lord, and take a seat on a silver-studded throne. Then bid the ushers pour out wine for all, so we can sprinkle drops to Zeus, the protector of those seeking shelter."

At this, Alcinous rose, grasped Odysseus by the hand and seated him on the throne beside him, in place of Laomedon, his favourite son. Food and drink were immediately brought for the guest, and wine poured into every cup. They all made their libation to Zeus, and when the stranger had eaten to his heart's content, the king rose and spoke.

"Listen, leaders of the Phaeacians. It is late now, and time that we were all in bed; but tomorrow morning, when we have called all the other nobles here, we shall give this unfortunate fellow the kind of welcome Zeus himself would want. We shall slay two oxen in honour of the gods and when we have all eaten and drunk our fill, we shall see about getting our guest back to his homeland and his loved ones – unless of course he is some god who has come to us as the immortals did in the old days, to share our feasts; for mankind are their descendants, just as the Cyclopes are descended from the Giants."

"Worthy Alcinous," Odysseus replied, "do not compare me with the gods, but only with other victims of terrible misfortune; for the immortals have dealt me crueller blows than mere mortals could devise. All I beg is that when dawn breaks you send me back to where I came from; for my one desire is to see my loved ones, and then I will die a happy man."

All who heard were touched, and filled with eagerness to help. When the noblemen had departed for their houses, Odysseus was left alone with Alcinous and Arete. She had recognized the clothes the stranger wore, having woven them herself, and said:

"Now, my guest, I will ask the first questions myself: where do you come from, how did you reach our land, and who give you the robe that you are wearing? For I believe you said you had been drifting on the sea."

"My queen," replied Odysseus, "it would be a hard task to tell you of all the troubles the gods have meted out to me, but I can answer how I came to be in this place, and your other questions." And he began to recount his sorry tale from the moment he had been washed up on Calypso's isle till the time the waves had cast him naked on the Phaeacian coast. He told her, too, of the good sense Nausicaa had shown on meeting him, and how she had given him the clothes that he now wore.

"Now I have told you everything, my lady," he said at last, "though it troubles my heart to dwell on all that I have been through."

"Stranger," Alcinous broke in, "you spoke of my daughter's good sense; but it was far from sensible of her to make you come here on your own."

Odysseus came to her defence in his usual shrewd way.

"Do not be angry with her, my lord," he protested. "It was I who wanted it that way, for fear that you might be displeased if you saw her in my company."

"Stranger," replied Alcinous, "I am never angry without reason. And as for you, you seem such a reasonable fellow, that I might wish you'd take the girl and become my son-in-law. But I know I cannot hold you here against your will, so tomorrow morning I shall see to it that everything is done to ensure you have a good, safe voyage and reach your homeland quickly. Our ships can sail as far as Euboea in a single day. But why tell you this? You will soon see for yourself what a splendid fleet I have, and what bold sailors to man it."

Next morning, at first light, everyone gathered in the great square of the city, where Alcinous presented Odysseus to all his nobles.

"Hear me, leaders of the Phaeacians," he cried. "This stranger, whose name not even I have learned, has fallen among us, driven by the waves, and begs our aid in returning to his country. No one who sought our help in making his way homewards has ever been denied it, so let us launch a good, fast ship and choose fifty of our strongest seamen, and tomorrow we shall send him on his way. Meanwhile, let us all go to the palace and offer him our hospitality – and send for the minstrel Demodocus, to lift both our hearts and the stranger's as he raises his sweet voice in song."

They all made for the palace, and the famous singer was summoned to appear, he to whom the Muse had given a gift and an affliction: she had endowed him with a splendid voice, but deprived him of his eyesight. A herald led him into the great hall and seated him upon a silver-studded stool by a tall pillar where he could rest his back. He hung his harp on a peg above his head and showed him where to stretch his hand when he wished to take it down.

They all fell to, and when they had eaten and drunk their fill, the spirit moved the heart of Demodocus to song. Taking down his harp, he began to sing of the Achaeans, of the time when they had just arrived in Troy and a fierce quarrel had broken out between Odysseus and Achilles. Agamemnon had rejoiced to learn of it, for an oracle had foretold that Ilium would fall when two of the best men in his army wrangled. But he was wrong to rejoice, for the prophesy referred not to this disagreement but to another, far more serious, which was destined to bring terrible suffering on both the Achaeans and the Trojans.

As he listened to the singer's words, Odysseus could not hold back his tears, and hid his face in the folds of his robe so the others would not see that he was weeping. When the song was ended, Odysseus wiped his eyes and bared his head. The nobles, however, were eager to hear the minstrel tell them more of Troy, and when Demodocus took up his harp again, Odysseus hid his face once more. His action passed unnoticed by all except Alcinous, who was seated close to him and heard his sobs. Out of kindness, he stood up and told the others:

"Now we've enjoyed a meal and a good song, let's go and try our strength at games and sports, so when our guest is safely back at home he can tell how we Phaeacians excel at running, jumping, wrestling and boxing."

At this hint they all got up and followed him out, and soon the games began. Many fine young men took part, among them the three sons of Alcinous, led by Laodamas, who won the boxing match. Turning to the others, the young victor suggested they ask whether Odysseus, too, would like to try his hand.

"He seems in good form," he added, "in spite of all he's been through, and even though there's nothing worse than the sea for wearing a man down, however strong he may be."

Everyone agreed, and so Laodamas invited Odysseus to take part in the games and put his troubles aside.

"Troubles like mine are not so easily forgotten," Odysseus replied. "Leave me be, I pray you, for all I want is to return to my own country."

Instead of respecting his wishes, Euryalus, a noble who had won the wrestling match, added rather thoughtlessly:

"No, stranger, you do not look like a man who would enjoy the games. I'd take you for a merchant, the kind that roam the seaways with their wares, grabbing what profits

..."People like you do not go in for sports"...

they can, and none too careful how they do it. People like you do not go in for sports."

Odysseus gave Euryalus an angry look and answered:

"I do not like your manner, sir. We know the gods do not grant all the graces to any man – handsome looks, good sense, strength and eloquence together. One man may not be much to look at, for example, but when he starts to speak, all those who hear hang on his every word and listen in wonder, as if he were a god. Another may be as handsome as they come, but his words are not crowned with grace. You are such a fine young fellow – a god would envy you your looks, but when it comes to brains, your mind is empty. You have offended me with your bad manners, and I would have you know I am not the kind of man you think. I've won my share of laurels in my time – but grief and bitterness have worn me down, what with all I've suffered in wars and on the seas. I still have some of my powers left to me, however, and so I'll try my hand – for you have cut me to the quick with your insulting comments."

Then he sprang to his feet, without even stripping off, and seized a heavy discus, much bigger than the one the Phaeacians had been throwing, and sent it spinning through the air with such velocity that it whistled in its flight. It soared into the sky and landed far beyond the other athletes' marks.

As it did so, Athena took the shape of a young man and

ran to mark the spot where it had fallen.

"A blind man could find the dent your discus made," she called out. "Why, it's so far and so deep, it stands out clear from all the others. Congratulations, stranger! No one here's a match for you."

Odysseus was so pleased to hear this that he forgot his troubles for a moment and flung a challenge to the Phaeacians:

"Beat that if you can, and I'll try an even longer throw next time. But I warn you, Euryalus has got my blood up now, so let's see who is man enough to take me on in wrestling, boxing, running or any other sport you care to name – except for Laodamas, of course; for I am not churlish enough to challenge my host in his own house, especially when he has shown such kindness to me. As for the rest of you, however, I'm ready to take on all comers, and I'll show whoever pits himself against me that I'm no mean hand when it comes to games. Give me a bow and I can pick out any target that I choose among the enemy host. Why, of all of us at Troy, only Philoctetes could outshoot me. As for javelins, there's not another man can match my throw. I am afraid of nothing but the foot-race, for years of tossing in the salty spray have slackened all my sinews."

The Phaeacians stood in silence after hearing all of this, till finally Alcinous spoke for them.

"You had every right to speak out as you did," he said. "You were insulted and wished to show your mettle. After all that we have heard, no other man will dare to say bad things about you! But listen now to what I have to say, so you will have a tale or two to entertain your friends when you have them to your hall for dinner. Zeus has given us Phaeacians many qualities. We may not be the first at wrestling and boxing, but there is no man who can rival us at running, rowing or anything that has to do with ships. As for dancing, singing and making merry, we adore these things – and we love fine clothes, a good warm bath and a comfortable bed! Come now, out with the best of our dancers, and let someone run to the palace to bring Demodocus his harp."

The harp was soon brought, and they all stood aside to make room for the dance. Demodocus stood in the middle, and the young men formed a ring around him with hands joined. With the first notes of the harp, they all stamped hard upon the ground and began to dance as if their feet flashed fire. Odysseus stood and gazed at them in wonder.

Next Demodocus sang of the immortals, telling how Ares was smitten with love for the bewitching Aphrodite, and how her husband Hephaestus had enmeshed the guilty couple in an invisible net.

Odysseus and the Phaeacians were delighted with the song. Then Alcinous asked two of his sons, Halius and Laodamas, to show the company their matchless skill at dancing. Taking a red ball, one of them bent his body back and threw it high into the air, while the other leapt and caught it before his feet touched ground again. After this game, they began to dance, rapidly exchanging places, while all around them the others clapped their hands so loud that the place echoed with the sound.

"These are sons any father could be proud of," Odysseus told Alcinous. "It makes me dizzy with wonder just to watch them."

Pleased with the compliment, the king turned to his nobles and said:

"Listen, my lords, there are twelve of you here and I make a thirteenth. Let us each bring a tunic and a mantle and add a talent of gold per man as well, and give all of it to our worthy guest. But as for Euryalus, he should beg the stranger's pardon and add another gift in recompense for his unfortunate remarks."

Everyone agreed, and Euryalus replied:

"Lord Alcinous, I willingly obey. I offer him this silver-handled sword, together with its ivory sheath." And with these words he unslung it from his shoulder and presented it to Odysseus, saying:

"Stranger, you are worthy of this gift. As for the harsh things that I said of you, let the wind carry them away. I wish you a safe journey home and hope you will soon be in your dear wife's sweet embrace, with all your sufferings in foreign lands a distant memory."

"My thanks, Euryalus," Odysseus replied. May the gods grant you all your heart desires – and may you never miss this sword which you have given me." With these words, he slung the silver-studded sheath over his shoulder.

The sun was setting in the west when the nobles brought their gifts. Alcinous' sons collected them and took them to the palace. The king returned home too, and as soon as he found Arete he told her:

"Bring the best trunk that we have, my dear, and my finest cloak and tunic. I want them for the stranger. Lay out the other gifts as well, so he may see them and rejoice. I shall present him this drinking-cup of solid gold, so he may sprinkle drops of wine in offering to the gods, and remember me as long as he may live."

Arete brought the wooden chest and spread out all the presents in front of it – and when Odysseus saw them he was delighted and moved by all their generosity. Then the queen instructed him to place the gifts inside it with his own hands and lash the lid down tightly. Last of all she ordered her servant-girls to help him bathe himself. Once he was clean and dressed in fresh new robes, he made his way to the great hall, where all the men were drinking wine. On his way, he happened to meet Nausicaa, who stopped him and said:

"Stranger, may the gods go with you – and wherever you may be, do not forget the girl who helped you in your time of trouble."

"You are a true daughter of your worthy father, Nausicaa," Odysseus replied. "May Zeus grant a quick dawning to the day of my return, and from my homeland I shall praise your name as if you were a goddess."

With these words, he went and took his place beside Alcinous.

The cooks carved the meat and served it, while the servants filled the cups with wine. A herald led in Demodocus and sat him with his back against a lofty pillar. Calling the herald over, Odysseus cut the best slice from his roast and told him to give it to the minstrel.

"Tell him it comes with a sad man's kindest wishes," he added, "for the Muse gives singers her especial love, and they deserve all men's honour and respect."

The singer was pleased by the stranger's gesture of respect, and even more pleased when Odysseus came to him after the feast and said:

"Demodocus, I admire you for the art Apollo and the Muse have taught you. You sing with such passion of the sufferings of the Achaeans before Troy that one might think you had lived through them yourself. Now I want to ask you a favour: sing to us of the wooden horse which Epeius made with the help of Athena, and which Odysseus contrived by stealth to be brought within the walls of lofty Ilium, bringing destruction down upon the Trojans. And if you tell all just as it happened, I will let the whole world know there is not another singer like you on this earth."

He had hardly finished saying this before Demodocus

began the song. His voice was like a god's, and Odysseus dissolved in tears, so strong were the emotions that assailed him. As before, Alcinous saw him weeping and called out to his nobles:

"It is time for the singer to lay his harp aside, for the tale he tells does not delight us all. From the moment that Demodocus began his song, our guest has not stopped sobbing. Some deep sorrow gnaws at him, it seems. Every grieving stranger is like a brother to us when we feel his sadness. So tell us, dear friend, what it is that troubles you – but first reveal your name, tell us what your father and dear mother called you, for there is no one in the world who does not have a name. Tell me the name of your homeland, too, and the village that you come from, so we can take you back there in the ship we have prepared, even though my father warned me that one day Poseidon would be angry with us for returning all lost travellers to their native lands, and would smash the ship we sent one in the moment it returned, and ring our island in with mountains. But, I brush such threats aside. Let the god do what he will, I say. Tell us, stranger, what regions have you wandered in, what cities have you seen? Of all the peoples you have been amongst, which were honourable and just and which were lawless? Finally, why do you weep and sigh when you hear of the sufferings of the Achaeans at Troy?"

Then Odysseus began his tale:

"My lord Alcinous, what can be better than a place where men live peacefully, and the king's guests sit at a loaded table, listening to a splendid singer? Yet in the midst of all this happiness, your heart is set on hearing my sad story, when even the memory of it brings tears into my eyes. Where shall I begin, where end, when the gods have heaped so many sorrows on me? First of all I shall reveal my name. I am Odysseus, the son of Laertes. All the world speaks of my shrewdness and quick wit, and the gods themselves have envied my renown. My home is Ithaca, the birthplace of brave fellows. It is a rocky island, but I love it. My wanderings have taken me across the world, yet I have never seen a sweeter sight than my own country. The lovely goddess Calypso tried to keep me by her in her cave and wanted me for a husband. The sorceress Circe held me prisoner in her gleaming palaces, and she, too, was eager for my love. Yet neither of them could turn my head, for there is nothing dearer in the world than home and kindred. But you must be waiting to hear of the obstacles Zeus placed in my path on my journey back from Troy.

With the Ciconians and the Lotus-Eaters

When my companions and I took ship and sailed, the wind carried us to the land of the Ciconians. They were our enemies, having fought against us with the Trojans, and we decided to sack their city, Ismaros. We caught them by surprise and took large quantities of loot and slaves, giving equal shares to all so there would be no cause for complaint. This done, I urged my comrades to leave while there was time, but the fools refused to listen, just sat down on the sand and began to ready lambs and oxen for the spit, swilling down unwatered wine as they did so. So, instead of setting sail, we spent the night upon the shore, where cruel fate had an ugly welcome waiting for us. The Ciconians from the city we had sacked fled to the mountains and warned others of their tribe, who were more numerous, bolder and more skillful in the arts of war. They came at dawn, more of them than the leaves upon the trees in spring. They drew up into groups at once, within attacking distance of the ships, some on foot and some in chariots. The signal was given, then suddenly they were all around us, lunging with their spears. We put up a brave defence and fought them stubbornly, shield to shield, holding them at bay throughout the day, although they outnumbered us by thousands. But by the time the sun was sinking in the west, the hour when weary oxen are unyoked from the plough, the Ciconians had got the upper hand. We lost six brave comrades from each ship, and the rest of us just managed to escape the jaws of death. Scrambling back on board, we ran up the sails, grieving for our lost companions – but we did not put out to sea till we had called the name of each of them three times.

We had not got far from shore when Zeus sent a savage

...On the tenth day we made land in the country of the
Lotus-Eaters...

north wind down upon our fleet, together with a fog which blotted out the sky. The ships were blown plunging along and the sails were torn to shreds by the violence of the gale. We hauled down what was left of them, seized the oars and turned our prows towards the shore again, to save ourselves from drowning. There we stayed for two whole days and nights, sewing our torn sails, and on the third day we climbed on board again and left. We had a good stern wind, and we were sure that it would blow us safely home; but as we were doubling Cape Maleas, we were caught by a strong northerly which pushed us back into the open sea.

Nine days we had the wind against us, and on the tenth we made land in the country of the Lotus-Eaters. We still did not know where we were. We disembarked to take on water, then sat down by the ships to eat. I sent three comrades to find out what kind of people lived in that place and before long, they came across some of the natives. They did no harm to my men, and only gave them some of their lotus fruit to taste – but as soon as they had done so they forgot about their homes and their companions and wanted nothing more than to stay in the land of the Lotus-Eaters and live off this magic fruit, which was as sweet as honey. We waited in vain for their return, for all thought of us had been wiped clean from their minds. In the end, I took a few companions and went and found them with the Lotus-Eaters. My scouts had completely forgotten who I was, and offered me some of the fruit they held, as if I were a passing stranger. Luckily, the gods opened my eyes for me and made me realize that if I ate I, too, would forget my country and my comrades. So, without wasting time on words, we hauled them off by force back to the ships. They wept like children all the way, but we pulled and prodded them along, and as soon as we got back I tied them up under the rowing-benches. Then I called out to my companions to jump on board and pull off with all speed, in case they, too, ate the lotus fruit and forgot where they had come from.

In the land of the Cyclopes

With heavy hearts we put back out to sea and within a few days reached a land inhabited by the Cyclopes, huge and fearsome giants with one eye in the middle of their forehead. They do not plough or sow the earth, for everything there grows by itself: wheat, barley, grapes and what you will. They never meet to discuss their common problems, and as for laws, they do not know what they are. They live apart, in caves high on the mountains, and each one concerns himself with his own affairs alone. They are completely indifferent towards their neighbours.

Beyond their harbour lies a lovely green island, empty of men but filled with wild goats which find rich grazing in its lush meadows. It has its own sheltered cove for ships, where you need no anchor-stones or hawsers but just beach your vessel as long as you like upon the shore and leave it till you feel like sailing off again. It's just a stone's throw from where the Cyclopes live, and yet they've never been across to it, nor anywhere else, for that matter, for they have no ships and do not like the sea.

We sailed into this bay at night. At its head there was a cave, with a spring of clear water gushing out beside it, and all around grew tall and shady poplars. We clambered over the thwarts and spent the remaining hours of darkness in that beautiful, safe place.

At dawn, we rose and set off in search of wild goats. The gods were with us and we had good hunting. I had twelve vessels and we killed enough for nine goats each, with one to spare, which the comrades awarded to my ship. We ate fresh meat all day, and drank sweet wine as well, for we had plenty left on board from the sacking of Ismaros. Just opposite we could see the land of the Cyclopes, and hear their voices mingling with the bleats of sheep and goats. Next day, I said to my companions:

"You stay here, and my crew and I will take our ship and sail across to see what kind of folks live there – whether they are wild and lawless or respect the gods and are kindly towards strangers."

So my crew and I climbed on board and we made our way over to the facing shore. Not far from the beach we saw a cave. It was tall and wide and round it flocks of sheep and goats lay resting.

Telling the rest of my companions to stay on board, I

chose twelve of the strongest and most daring and set off in that direction. With us we took a goatskin full of wine. It was so strong that you had to mix in twenty parts of water before it could be drunk, and when you did, such a sweet fragrance rose from the ruby liquid it was impossible to keep your lips from the cup – not that I took it for ourselves to drink, but because I knew that we were going to meet a huge and savage man who had nothing but evil in his heart.

We went to the cave while he was out grazing his sheep in the meadows. It was wide and lofty and ran deep into the mountain. Inside, there were even stone pens for the Cyclops' herds. In one corner were stacks of cheeses and in another great jars filled with whey and the empty tubs and pails he used for milking. My companions were terrified, and begged me to let them help themselves to some cheeses and a sheep and goat or two apiece and then be off. I ignored them, being curious to meet the Cyclops and see what he would give us of his own accord, rather than stealing from him. If only I had listened to my men! As it was, we just helped ourselves to a little of the cheese and sat down to wait for him.

When he arrived, he was carrying a huge load of firewood which he threw down onto the floor of the cave with such a crash that the whole place shook and we shrank back trembling into a dark corner. Next he drove in his ewes and began to milk them, leaving the rams and billy-goats outside. After that, he went to the cave entrance and picked up a rock so huge and heavy that twenty chariots could not have dragged it from its place; but he lifted it with ease with his two bare hands and blocked the entrance to the cave. Then he set the lambs under the mother sheep to suckle and made half the milk he had collected into cheese, keeping the rest to drink. When all his tasks were finished, he lit a fire. Its flames lit up the corner we were cowering in and he spotted us.

"Who are you fellows?" he roared, "and how did you get here? Have you come to trade, or are you here like pirates, ready to make off with other peoples' goods, to kill or to be killed?"

His angry words and deep, rough voice put fear into our hearts, but I managed to stand up and say to him:

"We are lost Achaeans, soldiers of the mighty Agamemnon, and we are trying to get home from Troy, but the gods have chosen to drive us off our course with contrary winds, and now we throw ourselves at your feet and beg your help. Give us food and shelter, as is the custom everywhere, and as almighty Zeus, the traveller's guardian, would wish."

He answered me with cruel words.

"You are a fool, my little friend, or else you come from so far off you have not heard that the Cyclopes do not give a damn for Zeus or any other god. Our strength is fearsome, and I, Polyphemus, son of Poseidon, am strongest of us all. Why, even the immortals are terrified of me! However, I may decide to take pity on you, if you just tell me where

..."Who are you fellows?" he roared, "and how did you
get here?"...

your ship is anchored — merely out of curiosity, you know."

He was trying it on, of course, but I wasn't to be fooled that easily.

"Alas, our ship is wrecked," I answered. "Poseidon smashed it on the rocks, and only I and these few friends escaped."

The giant said nothing in response to this. He simply looked my comrades over — and then did something hideous. His huge, hairy paws shot out, seized two of them, and beat their brains out on a rock the way you kill an octopus. Then he tore their lifeless bodies limb from limb and gobbled them, crunching bones and all. When he had wolfed them both, he lifted a whole pail of milk and swilled it down into his bottomless gut, while we groaned and lifted up our hands to Zeus in vain. Rubbing his great belly, he stretched and yawned, then sank down among the sheep and fell into a heavy slumber punctuated with hair-raising snores. My first instinct was to draw my sword and plunge it through his liver, but then I thought that even if I killed him we would not escape death's clutches, for there was no way we could shift the rock that blocked the entrance to the cave. So we waited for the dawn. When daylight came, he rose, relit the fire and milked the ewes and she-goats once again. He placed the young under their mothers' teats to suck, and when he had finished all his tasks, he seized two more of my companions, beat them to death against the ground and then devoured them. His belly filled, he went off to graze his flock, rolling the rock aside with ease, but immediately pushing it back again, so we were shut inside. While he was gone, I racked my brains to find a way of avenging ourselves upon this fearful monster and regaining our lost freedom, if Athena would grant my prayer.

Inside his cave, the Cyclops had a fresh-cut trunk of fir. Perhaps he'd intended to use it as a walking-stick once it had dried, but to us it seemed more like the mast for a ship with twenty oars. I cut off a good arm's length of this and gave it to my men to whittle down. When they had got it smooth, I sharpened one end to a point and thrust it into the embers of his fire to dry the sap out. When it was hardened, I hid it beneath the dung upon the floor, then told my comrades to cast lots to choose the ones who would join me in driving it into the Cyclops' eye. The lots fell to the men I would have chosen anyway – four of the strongest of them, and myself making a fifth.

When evening came, the Cyclops returned and carried out his usual tasks, then grabbed two of my crew once more and made his dinner of them. As he wiped his lips, I took a wooden bucket, filled it with the wine I had brought with me and offered it to him with both hands.

"Here you are, Cyclops," I called out, "have some wine to drink, now you have made a hearty meal of man-meat. Taste what a splendid drink I had on board my ship and perhaps you will take pity on me and help me to get home. But you're a heartless fellow. How can you expect anyone to visit you when you behave in such a savage fashion?"

Without a word, he snatched the wine and downed it in one gulp.

"Give me some more!" he begged, "and tell me what your name is. Then I will make you a present to be pleased with. We, too, make wine — but yours is better than the nectar of the gods."

I gave him more. He asked for a third draught, and once again I handed it to him. I could see that he was getting dizzy now and so I said:

"Cyclops, you asked what I am called, and promised me a gift, so I shall tell you what my name is. I am Nobody. Nobody is what I'm known as by my father, mother, friends and all."

That's what I said to him, and this is how the monster answered:

"When Polyphemus promises a present, he never goes back on his word; so here is mine to you, Mr Nobody, and a great favour it is, too: I shall eat you last of all!"

As he said this, his one eye closed, he sank heavily to the floor and began to snore and slobber and growl like a wild beast, spewing up wine and mangled gobbets of my comrades. Then I took our stake from its hiding-place and held its point over the fire till it glowed red, trying to bolster my companions' courage as I did so. I waited till it was so hot that it was on the point of bursting into flame, then took a good hold on it with the other four and plunged

"...Why are you last, you lazy creature?"...

the burning tip into the Cyclops' single eye with all the strength the gods had given us.

The giant howled in agony, and the cavern's rocky walls echoed and re-echoed with his screams. Out of his mind with pain, he hollered to the other Cyclopes to run and help him. We sprang back in alarm as he tore the sizzling stake out from his eye-socket and, thrashing his bleeding head from side to side, cried for assistance again and yet again. Hearing his frenzied roars, the other Cyclopes came hurrying to the cave.

"What is the matter with you, Polyphemus?" they asked bad-temperedly. "Why are you screaming out like this in the middle of the night and waking us all up? Have your flocks been stolen, or is someone trying to take your life by stealth or force? Tell us, who is it?"

"It's Nobody!" howled the Cyclops, "Nobody, I tell you!"

"Nobody?" they responded, "Well, if nobody is hurting you, then it must be some sickness sent down from the heavens, and the only one who can help you there is your father Poseidon, not us."

That's all the other Cyclopes had to say, and then they left. I laughed with all my heart to see how perfectly my trick had worked.

Moaning in distress, Polyphemus stumbled to the entrance, heaved aside the boulder and ran his hands throughout the flock as they made their way out of the cave, lest any of us escape that way. Poor fool! Did he think I wouldn't find a way of evading his clutches? I tell you, I ran through every cunning trick my mind could seize upon, for now it was our very lives that were at stake. Then it occurred to me that the best way to get out would be by hanging upside-down beneath the bellies of his rams, for there were some great fat ones in the cave, with shaggy fleeces. I separated them and tied them three abreast with long reeds from the Cyclops' couch, so my comrades could each hang from the middle one. One of the rams was even bigger than the others, and I got beneath him and took a firm grip on his shaggy flanks. My companions went through first. The Cyclops ran his fingers over the rams' backs, but how was he to see we were escaping him by hanging on beneath their bellies! Last of all came the ram I was, suspended from. Polyphemus recognized it by touch and asked, "Why are you last, you lazy creature? That's not your way. You were always first to leave the cave and find sweet grass to graze on by the stream. You were first to go in search of water, too, and first to come back to the fold at dusk. But now you've stayed till last to weep for the lost eye of your master, the eye that cursed Nobody put out when he'd fuddled me with wine. Ah, if only you could speak, then you could tell me where he's hiding from my wrath. You'd see how I would beat him on the rocks until his spirit fled his shattered corpse, and how the pain this Nobody has given me would be relieved."

Having said all this, he let the ram out. As soon as it was past the courtyard, I disentangled myself and ran to free my comrades. We were safe at last. Before making our way down to the ships, we drove some sheep off from the herd and took them with us. The others greeted us with joy and sadness mixed, and we all wept together for the companions we had lost. There was little time for grief, for we had to leave with all speed possible, but once we were a little way off shore I stood up in the bows and cried out at the top of my lungs:

"Hey, Polyphemus! Strangers were in your house and begged for help, but you did not hesitate to eat them. Now vengeance has fallen on you for your evil deeds!"

This made the Cyclops more furious than ever. In his rage, he broke off the whole top of a mountain and hurled it down on us. It narrowly missed our prow and sent up a huge column of spray, while the ship was flung backwards by its wash and would have fallen on the rocks if I had not staved it off with a long spear. Then I ordered my crew to grab hold of the oars and pull with all their might until we were in the open sea again and beyond the grasp of Charon. But once we had put twice the previous distance between us and the shore, I started shouting once again, so bitter did I feel about the companions we had lost.

"Don't be so foolhardy!" the others protested. "Why provoke such a fearsome monster? You saw the size of the rock he flung at us. We thought our end had come. Leave him be, in case he decides to throw another one this way."

But nothing could restrain me now, and I shouted out a second time:

"Hey, Cyclops! If anyone asks you who put out your ugly eye, tell him it was the man who conquered Troy: Laertes' son, Odysseus of Ithaca!"

And this is what he shouted back:

"Alas, all that was written has come true! A seer who lived here and told the Cyclopes' future for them warned me that some day I should be blinded by a fellow named Odysseus. But I imagined that Laertes' son would be a mighty giant like us, not the puny weakling who fuddled me with wine. Come back and be my guest, Odysseus, and I will ask my father Poseidon to give you his aid, for only he can send you safely homewards and cure my wounded eye."

That's what he said, and here is what I answered:

"Ah, if only I could drink your blood, and hurl you into the dark depths of Hades, where even Earthshaker could not find you and heal your goggle eye!"

In response to this, he cupped his hands and let out a great cry:

"Hear my plea, Earthshaker Poseidon! If you are truly my father and I your son, do not allow the son of Laertes to get back to his home. But if the fates have decreed that he shall see his house and kinsmen once again, then buffet him upon the seas for years, and when he does reach home at last, may it be alone, with all his comrades lost, his own ship wrecked – and may fresh troubles await him when he comes!"

With these words he sent another huge boulder spinning through the air and nearly smashed our steering-oar. Falling where it did, however, it pushed us further out to sea and so we soon got back to the desert island, where the crews of the other ships were waiting for us with sad and anxious faces.

When night fell, we lay down on the sand to sleep and in the morning we went on board and set sail, mourning the loss of our dear friends.

Ithaca within reach

Soon after leaving the country of the Cyclopes we reached Aeolia, the island home of the god Aeolus, who rules the winds. He lived in a bronze tower and had six sons and six daughters. He had married these sons to the girls, and they all lived happily together with their parents. Each day the palace echoed with their songs, and at night they all slept snuggled up in couples in their fine, carved beds. I spent a whole month as a guest in Aeolus' shining palace and he loved to hear my stories of the endless travails of the Achaeans before they finally took Troy. When we decided it was time to leave, he slaughtered a great ox and from its hide he made a bag. In it he shut up all the winds and gave it me to watch over on my ship, after first tying up its mouth with a silver cord, so tightly that not a breath of air could escape. There was one wind he left out, however. This was Zephyrus, which blew steadily from the west and drove our ships on a homeward course. But it was not our destiny to reach home yet, alas. Nine days and nights we sailed along, and on the morning of the tenth we sighted Ithaca. We got so close that we could even see smoke rising from the chimneys of the houses. Yet I was so sleepless and exhausted that I could not hold out till landfall and I nodded off. All through the voyage it had been I who held the rope that kept our sail taut. I had not wanted to entrust it to another's hands in my anxiety to get us back among our own folks with all speed. The moment my eyes closed, my comrades began to whisper that the bag which Aeolus had given me had gold in it.

"How does Odysseus manage it?" they said. "Wherever he goes, he wins men's hearts. Look how much loot he's brought back with him from Troy, while we who fought alongside him are coming home with empty hands. Now Aeolus has gone and given him more still. Let's see how lucky he was this time, and how much gold and silver's in the bag."

So the fools untied the silver cord and brought calamity upon themselves and me. The winds came rushing out and stirred up a great storm which drove our vessels back into the open sea. I woke up, and when I realized what had happened I almost decided to jump into the waves and drown, to put an end to all my miseries. But at last I took a hold upon myself and decided to face this new evil with whatever strength was left in me. For days we struggled against the storm, until the gale drove us back again to the island of Aeolus. We went ashore, drank a little water and had a bite to eat, and then I took two companions and went up to the palace. We found Aeolus feasting with his wife and children, and when we entered, he called out in astonishment:

"What brings you here again, Odysseus? What ill-luck dogs your foot-steps? Didn't we send you back to the place your heart was longing for?"

"Alas," I answered, "Sleep and my comrades got the better of me. But come, brothers, help me again, since you have the power."

I had been sure they would take pity on me. Instead, Aeolus cried out angrily:

"Out of my sight, you accursed creatures! I will not sin again by helping men the blessed gods have marked as enemies. Be gone with you, and don't show your faces here again!"

And with these harsh words he turned us unfortunate visitors out of his house. With heavy hearts, we climbed on board the ships, and my comrades slumped down over the oars with neither hope nor courage left.

Disaster in the harbour of the Laestrygonians

Six days we travelled blind, and on the seventh we sighted land. It was the country of the Laestrygonians. We found a good closed harbour there, surrounded by tall cliffs. My comrades moored their vessels well inside, but I left mine beyond the harbour entrance and moored it to some rocks. When we disembarked, we climbed the tallest of the cliffs to see the countryside which lay around. It seemed strange to me, for while there was no farmland to be seen anywhere, smoke was rising from far off and a carttrack led into a wood. I sent three men to find out what kind of folks lived in these parts, and they took the road which led towards the forest. After some time a city came in sight. Near its gate there was a spring where a great tall girl was going for water with a pitcher in her hand. They asked her who was king of this country and said that they would like to meet him. The girl, who was none other than the king's daughter, showed them where her father's palace lay and then bent down to fill her pitcher. The three comrades went on to the palace, but as soon as they entered their eyes fell upon a woman as huge as a mountain, and they were terrified. Without saying a word to them, she sent for her husband, Antiphates, who was at a council-meeting in the city square. He came in haste, but with murderous intentions; for he, too, was a giant, and a fearsome one. The moment he laid eyes on my three crewmen in the palace he stretched out a huge hand, snatched one up and ate him. The other two took to their heels, but Antiphates gave a terrifying roar which set the other Laestrygonians on their trail. Thousands of giants poured into the streets and made hotfoot for the harbour. As soon as they saw the ships they began to shower huge rocks down on them. It was a scene of utter turmoil. All were smashed to splinters and my unfortunate sailors carried off to make a supper for the Laestrygonians. Luckily for me, my vessel had been moored outside the harbour, so I slashed through the hawsers with my sword and yelled out to my crew to row for all their lives were worth. They were even more terrified than I was, and whipped the sea into a boiling foam as they heaved madly at the oars. Soon we were far from shore. My own ship was safe, but all the others had been lost.

With the sorceress Circe

Shattered by the disaster which had befallen us, we sailed into the unknown. Eventually we reached the island of Aiaia, the home of Circe, daughter of the sun-god Helios. We dragged our ship up on the shore and sat there for two days, mourning our dead comrades. At dawn upon the third day I climbed a mountain peak and spied smoke rising above a wooded hill. I was in half a mind to walk there to find out where we were and whether there was any chance of help for us, but I held back for fear of what I might encounter. Besides, my first duty was to find food for the crew, since we had not eaten a bite in days. Just as I was wondering how I was to do so, what should come out of the forest but a great fat buck! Thanking whatever god had set him in my path, I hurled my spear and killed him. Then I heaved the heavy beast across my shoulders and brought him down to my companions, saying:

"In spite of all the troubles that beset us, we shall beat Charon yet. No man dies before his hour has come. Quick, skin this fellow and get him ready for the spit. Hunger has gnawed at our entrails long enough!"

With joyful faces, they got a fire alight and roasted the buck, and all day we ate, drank and regained our strength.

"The time has come to decide what we must do," I told them. "When I climbed up to that mountain-top, I saw that there was sea all round. But the island that we're on is not deserted, for somewhere in the distance I saw smoke rising from among the trees. All we need to do is go there to find out where we are."

My comrades' hearts sank at my words. They remembered the disaster which had struck us in the country of the Laestrygonians, and what had happened when we went to meet the Cyclops. They were so discouraged that they wept at the thought of what worse things might befall them. But nothing comes of tears, and so I split them up into two groups and appointed brave Eurylochus, a relative of mine, as the leader of the first, while I stayed with the other. Then I threw two lots into a helmet to see which group would go out and explore the island. As I shook them, out leapt the lot of Eurylochus.

He set off with his team all looking very miserable, while we stayed back to guard the ship, with fear in our hearts. They pushed on across the island and on a wooded rise they found the palace of the daughter of the Sun. It was built of polished marble which gleamed in the bright morning light. Around it padded lions and wolves, but they did not harm the party, for Circe, who was immortal and a mighty sorceress, had tamed them all with magic potions. When they reached the door they heard a sweet female voice singing inside.

"Let's give her a shout, whoever she is," one of them suggested. They called out and she ceased her singing and came to open the door. It was Circe herself, a lovely and imposing goddess. She invited them in and they all entered except Eurylochus, who feared some evil. She begged them to be seated, then offered them a porridge of cheese and honey mixed with flour and wine. But into it she slipped some magic herbs. When they had eaten, she struck them with a wand, led them outside and herded them into pens. What happened next was even worse: their voices turned to grunts, their noses lengthened into snouts and bristles sprouted from their bodies till they became like pigs in every way, save that she left their minds untouched, to make their sufferings still more bitter.

Eurylochus waited in vain for his companions, and when he realized some great harm must have come to them he took to his heels so that he at least would be saved. By the time he reached the ship he was half dead from terror and trembling so violently he could not get a single word out of his lips. We pressed him anxiously, until at last he found his voice again and told us that while out scouting they had come to a tall palace where a terrible witch dwelled, and that his comrades had simply vanished the moment they set foot in it.

As soon as I heard this I buckled on my sword, picked up my bow and ordered Eurylochus to come along and point me out the way. Instead of obeying, he threw himself at my feet and started begging not to go.

"Leave me here, I implore you, and do not even think of going there alone, for I know you won't come back, far less bring any of our companions with you. Get us out of this accursed place while there's still time. Those of us left still have some chance of escape!"

His cowardice disgusted me, but I only said:

"Stay here, then, Eurylochus, and eat and drink beside the ship – but as for me, go to Circe's palace I must and go I will." And with these words I set off alone into the forest.

On the way, who should stop me but Hermes, in the guise of a handsome youth. He grasped me in a friendly fashion by the arm and spoke with concern in his voice.

"Where are you going, you poor fellow, all alone and in strange country? Off to see Circe and her herds of swine, no doubt. I warn you, it's pigs she's turned your comrades into, and a pig she'll turn you into, too, when you try to set them free. But I will save you from the terrible fate she has in store for you. Do you see that plant that's growing from the rock? It will protect a man from any evil. First you must listen, though, while I tell you of all her cunning tricks and how you must respond to them. To start with she will give you porridge in which she has sprinkled some of her magic herbs, but they will not take hold on you, thanks to the powers this good plant wields. Next she will come to strike you with her wand, but you must draw your sword and threaten to fall on her and kill her. In her terror, she will first try to soothe you with sweet words, then offer to let you sleep with her. Do not refuse if you wish to rescue your companions, but before you do so, make her swear a solemn oath by all the gods that she will do you no harm and will not rob you of your manhood when you lie down by her side."

Having said this, the wing-footed god pulled the plant out from its crevice in the rock. It had pure white flowers and a black root so tough no human hand could have dislodged it. The gods can do all things, however.

When he had presented it to me he left for Olympus, and I stood there thinking of my comrades and how I could release them. On reaching the palace, I struck the door and

..."How can you ask me to be tender with you, Circe, when you have turned my comrades into swine?"...

called out. Circe came and opened to me. She led me in and seated me on a handsome silver-studded throne with a footstool set before it. Then she prepared the gruel Hermes had warned me of and brought it to me in a golden bowl. She had thrown in magic herbs to accomplish her evil purpose, but I drank the mixture without flinching because I knew her arts would not take hold on me. As soon as I had drunk, she lifted up her wand to strike, snarling, "Now run and join your companions in the pig-sty!" But I drew my sword and fell on her as if I had murder in my heart. She let out a loud shriek and flung her arms around my knees. Sobbing with terror, she asked me:

"Who are you? How could you swallow such a potion and not be bewitched, when no man has withstood my magic arts till now? Ah, now I understand: you must be Odysseus, he whom Hermes warned me once would pass this way on his return from Troy. Come now, put up your keen blade in its sheath. Lie down with me upon my bed and love me."

"How can you ask me to be tender with you, Circe, when you have turned my comrades into swine and are trying now to trick me, too, and rob me of all my strength? I shall never sleep with you unless you swear the most solemn oath you know that you will never make another evil attempt against me."

She accepted my terms, and after I had seen her make the binding promise I demanded, I lay with her on her silken bed.

When we arose, we found a feast set out for us. Four wood-nymphs worked in Circe's service, and it was they who had prepared the tasty dishes and laid the table for us. They filled our golden goblets with sweet wine, and when they showed their mistress by a nod that all was ready, she took me by the hand and led me in to eat, pulling up a fine carved chair for me to sit on. My thoughts were elsewhere, though, and everything around seemed black to me.

When Circe saw me slumped in my seat with a long face, not even reaching out my hand to the delicious food upon the table, she leaned towards me and asked in a concerned voice:

"Odysseus, why are you sitting there so sad and silent? You have a splendid meal in front of you and you do not even touch it. Do you believe that I'm still trying to work you harm, perhaps? If that is so, fear not – for I have sworn not to by all that is most solemn to me."

Here's what I said in answer to her words:

"What man worth his salt could eat and drink when he knew his comrades had been turned into pigs and were penned up in a sty within a stone's throw of this table? If you want to make me happy, unbind the spell you have cast on my companions, and let me see them once again."

When I said this, she led me out of the palace and went to open the gate of the sty. Then all the pigs came trotting out, and by their sad looks I knew them for my comrades and my heart was torn with pity. She took a magic ointment and rubbed a little of it on each bristly head – and lo and behold they were transformed into men once more, but even younger and more handsome than they'd been before. They ran up and clasped me by the hands, sobbing with relief. It was such a touching scene that Circe herself was moved by it and said:

"Go down to the ship, Odysseus. Pull it up on shore and hide your gear in a cave. Then all of you come back here and stay with me."

Her frank look told me this was no plot she was laying, so I set off for the shore, but when I got there I found the rest of my companions weeping anxious tears. You can't imagine their joy when they set eyes on me! They were like calves at sundown when they see their mothers returning to the byre and rush towards them with such bellowing and shoving no force on earth can hold them back. That's how my sailors were with me, rushing wet-eyed into my arms the moment that I hove in sight! You'd have thought they were already back in rocky Ithaca, the way they carried on.

"Come on," I told them, "pull the ship up on the beach and let's hide our tackle in these caves. Once that's done, we're off to join our comrades who are wining and dining in Circe's palace."

They all obeyed except Eurylochus, who turned on them and cried:

"Are you out of your minds, you fools? If we set foot in

Circe's house she'll turn us all into pigs and wolves and lions to keep watch over her domain. Look how we paid for Odysseus' last piece of madness, when we followed him into the Cyclops' cave!"

His defiance sent the blood straight to my head. Relative or no, I would have drawn my sword and cut him down if the others hadn't held me back by saying:

"Come on, chief, leave the poor fellow be! Set him to guard the ship, and lead the rest of us to Circe's palace!"

Soon after, we set off. Not even Eurylochus stayed behind, for my display of anger had thoroughly cowed him.

We reached the palace and found our companions sitting at table. There were tearful embraces all round and the goddess, filled with pity for us, came and told me:

"Son of Laertes, listen. You have shed enough tears, all of you. I am well aware of all the troubles and setbacks you have suffered. Stay in my palace till you have recovered. How can a smile light up your bitter faces with all the memories of your torments fresh inside you? When the time comes and you want to leave again, I shall place no obstacles in your path, but on the contrary, I shall help you on your way."

I liked the way she spoke, and so, for my comrades' sake, decided we would stay. They were all delighted, for if there was one thing they all needed it was rest and relaxation.

Voyage to Hades

Those were happy days we spent in Circe's palace. Eat, drink and be merry was the order of the day, and merry we were, I can tell you! The weeks and months rolled by, and soon it was a year since our arrival. Then someone spoke to me of home. One word was all he needed. A desperate longing for my house and dear ones suddenly welled inside me. When night fell and the rest had gone to bed, I knelt and clasped the goddess round the knees and begged her:

"Oh, Circe, the time has come for you to keep the promise that you made. Send me back home, where my heart is. My companions are sick with longing, and it's more than I can bear to see them."

"Odysseus," she replied, "I will not keep you any longer if it is your wish to leave. But fate has one last voyage in store for you, more thankless than any you have made so far. You must go down to Hades and ask the seer Teiresias to tell you the way back."

I knelt there in stunned silence. It was some time before I found the strength to ask:

"How can I get to Hades when I'm still alive? Who will guide me there? Has anyone ever made the voyage by sea?"

"When the gods will it, all is possible," Circe replied. "Set sail, and Boreas the north wind will take you to the ocean's limit. There you will find a sea-shore backed by willow trees and poplars. This forest belongs to Persephone, the queen of Hades. Beach your ship there and press on till you reach the spot where the Acheron meets the waters of the Styx. There dig a trench a fathom wide and pour libations of honey, milk, water and wine into it. Sprinkle all these with flour then sacrifice a black ram and a ewe to Teiresias, making sure that their blood flows in to join the other liquids in the trench. When you do so you will see the countless hosts of the dead approaching you – but do not let them draw near until you have spotted the shade of Teiresias and had a word with him."

With a sinking heart I went to break her news to my companions. It threw them into black despair, but terrified as they were, they knew there was no other choice.

One of our company, young Elpenor, had spent the night on the flat roof of the palace. Our noisy preparations for departure jerked him awake. Still fuddled with sleep, he missed his footing and tumbled to his death. Here was yet another comrade gone, but we could not let it delay our departure. Circe had already brought a black ram and a ewe to make the sacrifice, so we took them on board and set sail.

As Circe had foretold, our ship was guided by the wind. After a long voyage we reached the limits of the ocean, where the land of the Cimmerians lies swathed in mist and hidden by black clouds. Dropping anchor, we took the sheep ashore and drove them to the place she had told us of. I dug a pit there with my sword and poured in the

libations of honey, water, milk and wine. Next I tossed in a
few handfuls of barley meal. Finally I sacrificed the animals and let their blood trickle into the trench. As it flowed,
the souls of the dead began to gather round, jostling one
another in their eagerness to drink the blood of sacrifice
and regain some memory of who they were and what fate
had befallen them. I drew my sword and kept them all at
bay, waiting to catch sight of Teiresias. Yet as it chanced,
the first shade to approach was that of Elpenor, for in our
haste to leave Aiaia we had left him where he lay. He
begged me to go back and bury him, to let his soul find
rest. It broke my heart to see him there and I promised we
would carry out his wish. Next I saw the spirit of Anticleia,
my mother, whom I had last seen alive on Ithaca. I wept to
see her there among the dead, but I knew I must not let her
drink the blood and recognize me before I had seen the
shade of the soothsayer Teiresias, who even in Hades had
kept his powers of memory, thought and prophesy.

At last I saw him. Holding a golden sceptre, he came up
to me and said:

"Son of Laertes, what do you seek in gloomy Hades?
Draw back from the pit and let me drink some blood, so I
can tell you all you need to know."

I moved aside and he knelt down to drink. When he got
up again he told me:

"A cruel and weary voyage still lies ahead of you, for
you have angered the god Poseidon by putting out the eye

..."A cruel and weary voyage still lies ahead of you"...

of his son, the Cyclops Polyphemus. However, you can still get home with all your comrades provided you do not disturb the oxen of the sun-god Helios, which graze upon the island of Thrinacia. Eat any of them, and it will cost you both your ship and crew. Even if you do not go down with them, you will only find your way to Ithaca again after long and desperate adventures, and when you do, it will be alone, and in a ship which is not yours. Your troubles won't end there, for inside your very house you will have a hard and bloody struggle against evil, shameless men who have been making free with all your stocks of food and wine while they quarrel over your wife's hand. Each one of them must meet the death that he deserves, some from your arrows and others by your spear."

The great seer told me many other things, besides – how I must make one last, long journey far inland, till I reached a place whose people did not know the sea, yet how it would be from the sea death finally came upon me, though swiftly and in honour, among my own dear people.

When the soothsayer had finished, my mother approached. Once she had drunk of the blood she remembered the old days and told me of all that had taken place on Ithaca. When I learned that she had pined away and died because I had been gone so many years, my grief was more than I could bear. Three times I tried to fold her in my comforting arms, and three times she slipped through them like the shadow of a dream.

Then I saw many other shades whom I had known in life. I spoke with Agamemnon, who wept as he recounted his murder by Aegisthus and the faithless Clytemnestra on his return from Troy. As I listened, broken-hearted, the spirit of Achilles came flitting up to me.

"Son of Laertes!" he exclaimed, "Descended into Hades, eh? – and still alive! After this coup, what's left for you to achieve?"

"I did not make this voyage to bring me glory," I replied. "No, Achilles, I came here to consult the seer Teiresias, for I have been tossed this way and that upon the seas for years, and cannot find my way back home. And if you speak of glory and achievement, there was no man on earth more fortunate than you. All honoured you while you were alive, and even in the kingdom of the dead you wield great power."

"Ah, Odysseus!" his shade sighed. "Do not try to console me. I'd a thousand times rather see the light of day again, even as some poor villager, than rule here in Hades. But tell me what you know of my son Neoptolemus. Did he go to the war and take a leading place? And what of my father? Is he still king in Phthia, or is it as I fear – do worthless men look down on him in his old age? If only I could go back for a moment to the house where I was born, and then you'd see the colour drain from the faces of those bullies who make a misery of his declining years!"

I had no news to give him of old Peleus, but I told of

Neoptolemus' brave feats at Troy and his heart swelled with a father's pride!

Next Patroclus, Antilochus and many others came up and spoke to me. Only great Ajax, the son of Telamon, stood resentfully aloof. Even here he could not forget that it was I who had won the dead Achilles' arms from him – and would I never had, seeing what a splendid man the dark earth swallowed up in consequence. Gently, I asked him if we might be friends again. It was Zeus alone who was to blame, I said, with the bitter hatred he had shown towards the Danaid cause.

But he turned on his heel and left me without answering.

I saw other well-known faces down in Hades, but by now I was anxious to leave, for the spirits' cries were swelling to an uproar and I was terrified that a Gorgon's head might suddenly appear and turn us into stone. I called out to my comrades to follow me back to the ship; we scrambled aboard, hauled up the sail and set off once again for Circe's island.

The bewitching Sirens' song

When we reached Aiaia, our first task was to bury Elpenor. We gathered wood and placed him on the funeral pyre together with his weapons. As the flames consumed his body, we wept bitter tears of grief. Then we raised a tall mound over his ashes and planted his rowing-oar upon its summit.

When we had finished, Circe came with her serving-girls, who spread a meal for us.

"Today you must eat and rest," the noble goddess told us, "for tomorrow you set off again. Fear not, though – I shall warn you what you must watch out for, and how to guard against the dangers you will meet upon your way."

We ate and drank, and when night fell and my comrades went off to their beds, Circe drew me aside.

"You will encounter many hazards before you reach your home, Odysseus," she told me. "Fearful obstacles lie in your way." And one by one she counted off the dangers I would face and how I was to overcome them. First she told me of the terrible Sirens, whose song bewitches all who sail within sound of their island. Next she warned me of the towering Planktes, huge moving rocks which would bar my passage; and then she spoke of Scylla and Charybdis, two fearsome monsters which lie in wait athwart a narrow strait and exact a hideous toll of all who pass between. Finally, like Teiresias, she cautioned us against eating any of Helios' oxen, if we wished to see our homes again.

The goddess spoke on and on, and before I realized it night had faded into dawn. When its pink flush spread over the horizon, Circe gave me a tunic and a cloak to wear and dressed herself in a long white robe, throwing a fine-spun veil over her face and clasping a beautiful gold belt about her waist.

The time for our departure came. The goddess accompanied us down to the ship and when we arrived I told my comrades to climb aboard and cast off. Once I had joined them, they sat down at the benches, seized the oars and quickly rowed us out of harbour. A little way off shore we hauled up sail, a fair breeze filled it and our ship sliced swiftly through the waves. It was a feeling to lighten a man's heart, but mine was heavy with the news I had to break to my poor comrades.

"Hear what I learned from Circe, who knows more than the mightiest gods. We must now sail past the island of the Sirens, bird-women whose sweet voices seduce all those who sail within sight of their lair. Whoever listens to their song will never again set eyes on home or loved ones but leave his bones to bleach upon their island, along with those of all the others who heard and were bewitched. To escape their clutches, you must block your ears with wax. So Circe told me, only I may be allowed to hear their song, but you must tie me so tightly to the mast that I cannot move an inch. If I cry out and beg to be released, do just the opposite: bind me even tighter."

As I was explaining all these things to them, the island of the Sirens appeared on the horizon. The wind dropped, and my comrades gathered up the sail and sat waiting at the oars. Then I took a lump of wax, cut it into small pieces, rolled them between my palms in the warm sunshine till they had softened, and plugged the ears of my companions.

..."Come, glorious Odysseus, pride of the Achaeans, pause here and listen enthralled to our sweet harmonies"...

When I had finished, they stood me up against the mast and bound me hand and foot, tugging the knots tight. Then they sat down at the oars again and the sea foamed at our prow as we skimmed across the waves towards the island. As we drew close, the Sirens spotted us and took up their lovely song, calling out in seductive voices:

"Come, glorious Odysseus, pride of the Achaeans, pause here and listen enthralled to our sweet harmonies, for no man ever sails this way without first drawing close to hear us, then voyaging on delighted doubly – both by our songs and by our secret knowledge. We know all you endured before you conquered lofty-towered Troy. We see all that happens on the face of this fruitful earth, and all things that are yet to come."

Their lovely song went on, and I was so desperate to get closer and hear more that I appealed to my comrades to untie me. They only pulled all the harder at their oars, while Perimedes and Eurylochus got up and bound me tighter still, despite my pleading. Once they were past, and their voices could no longer reach us, my faithful friends took out the wax which plugged their ears and released me from my bonds.

Between Scylla and Charybdis

We may have got safely past the Sirens, but my mind was already filled with dark forebodings about the much worse obstacles Circe had told me lay ahead.

'Once you leave the Sirens' island,' she had warned, 'you will have two sea-routes open to you. Both are highly dangerous – and it is you who must decide which one is safer for your ship and crew. First listen, though, to the horrors each one holds: in one you will see two massive rocks which open and close. The gods call them the Plank-tes. Not even birds can fly between them, except Zeus' doves when they go to bring ambrosia for the gods. Even then the rocks crush one of them each time, though Zeus always puts another in its place. If any ship dares risk the passage, then the sea fills with wreckage and smashed bodies, tossed on the angry storm-waves. In the other strait you will also see two rocks. One soars up to the heavens, and its jagged peak is swathed in black clouds, no matter what the season. A man could never reach its summit, even if he had twenty arms and legs, so steep and slippery is its surface. Half way up there is a cave, but even the strongest archer could not hit it from the sea. In its depths dwells Scylla, a hideous monster with a spine-chilling bark. No god would want to set eyes on her, let alone a man. She has twelve legs and six long, writhing necks on each of which is set an ugly head with three dense rows of deadly fangs. She lurks there in her hole and thrusts her snaky throats out from its entrance. They cast about above the waves in search of prey: dolphins and dogfish or any other morsel which the sea is rich in. No captain ever boasted that he passed that way unscathed, for each head snatches a sailor from the deck. The other rock is lower, and not a bow-shot from the first. At its edge there stands a fig-tree with dense foliage. In its shade sits Charybdis, a monster yet more terrible than the first. Three times a day she sucks up all the sea around her and sends it spouting out with terrifying force. Woe betide whoever happens to be there when Charybdis swallows up the waves, for even Poseidon the Earthshaker does not have the power to resist her. My advice to you would be to hold your course on Scylla's side, even if she snatches half a dozen of your men, rather than all go down together.'

'Suppose I manage to slip past Charybdis,' I suggested then, 'couldn't I attack Scylla as she was coming down to grab my men?'

'You hot-head!' she replied. 'Fighting and war is all you ever think about, Odysseus. Would you even set yourself against the gods? For Scylla is no mortal creature, but a savage, hideous monster no human strength can stand against. It's no use playing the hero with an invincible creature such as her. Just slip by as quick as you know how or else I'm afraid she'll snatch up twice as many of your comrades if you turn and make a fight of it. All you can do is offer up a prayer as you row by to Crataeis, her mother, who bore her to bring evil on the world, and then she will not let her strike a second time.'

I was still thinking of that all-night conversation we had

...Charybdis sucked the sea in with terrifying force...

held way back on Circe's island, when we suddenly beheld
a great foaming wave which reared itself sky-high, and
heard a hollow boom. The oars slipped from the terrified
sailors' grasp, the ship slowed to a halt and I ran forward to
spur on the crew.

"Brothers!" I cried, "We are no strangers to peril. What
we see here is no worse than what we suffered in the
Cyclops' cave, and I don't think you will ever forget whose
resourcefulness and courage got you out of there. So take
the oars again, my friends, and pull with all your might.
And you, steersman, keep our head well away from that
boiling foam and hug close to the cliffs. Don't let her drift
in the other direction, or we'll all be drowned."

That's all I said. I made no mention of Scylla, lest they
drop the oars again and huddle in the hold for shelter.
Ignoring Circe's advice to avoid risking any attack, I seized
two sharp-tipped spears and ran forward to await the
hideous beast's appearance. Search as I might, I saw no
sign of her, and my eyes were beginning to tire from
peering up into the dark depths of the cave. We entered the
channel heart in mouth, with Scylla's cliffs looming up an
oar's length from our side, while just over to our port
Charybdis sucked the sea in with terrifying force, dragging
it whirling, roaring down until the black sand on the bottom
was laid bare. Then she spewed it out again, dancing and
bubbling like boiling water in a cauldron with a blazing fire
beneath. Panic took hold of my companions. Their faces

turned a sickly yellow and they waited, trembling, for the end to come. And as we stared in awestruck horror at Charybdis, Scylla swooped down unseen upon our ship with her six heads. In a flash she seized six crewmen, those with the strongest arms, and the bravest lads in battle. Jerking my glance upwards, I saw them being drawn up into the sky, flailing their limbs and calling out my name for the last time. As we slipped past, the monster flung them against the jagged rocks which lined her cave and started to devour them. They screamed aloud and threw their arms out in a despairing plea for help. In all my years of war and voyaging, my eyes had never seen a sight more pitiful.

The cattle of Helios

When we were past the rocks and had escaped the terrors of Charybdis and Scylla we soon came to Thrinacia, the cool and clear-skied isle of Helios. From over the water we could hear the bleat of sheep and oxen lowing, for it was the evening hour, when animals return to the fold.

Then I recalled the words of the seer Teiresias, and what Circe had warned us against, as well, so I told my comrades:

"You remember what the blind soothsayer said to us, my friends, when we sailed this ship to Hades. Now I must add what Circe told us, too.

On this island, Helios' two daughters, Phaethusa and Lampetia, watch over their father's sheep and cattle as they graze. There are seven herds of oxen and as many again of sheep, with fifty beasts in each. That is their number, and it never changes – for these animals neither give birth nor die. If we do not touch them we shall get home, whatever desperate adventures still await us; but if we kill so much as one of them, we shall all meet our deaths upon the wild sea. That is why our wisest course would be not to set foot on the sun-god's isle at all."

When my companions heard these words they looked as if their hearts would break, and Eurylochus retorted angrily:

"You are a hard and stubborn man, Odysseus! Have you no thought for our weariness? You must have a heart of iron if you will not even let us go ashore to eat a little bread and stretch out on the sand till our hunger and exhaustion pass. Do you want us to sail on into open sea by night, when you know that darkness brings down the worst storms? What shall we do if the weather breaks and a sudden squall comes from the north to sink our ship? Let us obey the dictates of the night, I say, and only put out into the broad sea again when morning comes."

To a man, they sided with him and not with me. I realised then that we should not escape disaster.

"Eurylochus, you force me to relent, since I am only one against you all. However, I insist you swear a solemn oath that you will not lay a finger on a single animal, but only eat the food which Circe gave us."

After they had given this promise we sailed in and dropped anchor in a bay which had a spring of sweet running water. Wading ashore, we all sat down to eat. Our hunger satisfied, we remembered the comrades whom Scylla had snatched from us and we lamented them until at last sleep overcame our tired bodies. Shortly before dawn, we were awakened by a violent storm. The sky was hidden by black clouds and the sea whipped into sudden fury. We hauled the ship up on the beach and hid it in a cave to protect it from the savage wind. When all was safely stowed, I said to my companions:

"Listen, lads, we've food enough on board. There's bread and wine and we need lack for nothing. So don't any of you think of stealing Helios' oxen – for he's a god who sees and hears all from his post on high."

That's what I told them, and again they all agreed with me. But that gale raged on for a whole month, so wildly we did not dare so much as stick our noses from the cave. As long as our stocks of bread and wine held out we managed well enough but once these were exhausted my comrades had to brave the storm in search of food. They ate shellfish, birds and whatever else they could lay their hands on, yet they were still half-starved. Then I slipped away from the men and went up into the island to beg the gods to unbar our way home. I washed my hands and offered up my prayer. When I had finished, I sat down in the shade of an oak tree, and the gods poured sweet sleep into my eyes.

While I was slumbering far from my companions, Eurylochus seized the opportunity to give them the worst advice they could have heard.

"My poor, suffering friends," he said, "all deaths are bitter, but none is worse than starving. So I say, let's round up the finest of the cattle and sacrifice them to the gods. Whenever we get back to Ithaca we can raise a splendid temple to Helios and fill it with handsome offerings. Even if he's angry, and decides to sink our ship, I'd rather go down with a mouthful of salt water than slowly shrink into a bag of skin and bones half-way across the world from home."

His speech was greeted with applause. They drove off the best cattle and offered them to the gods on Olympus, scattering oak leaves on their victims for want of barley-meal. When the beasts were slaughtered and skinned, they chopped off the thighs and placed the wrapped joints on a fire, sprinkling them with water because they had no wine to perform the ceremony. Once these and the innards had been cooked and eaten, they cut the other pieces up and stuck them on spits to grill over the embers.

It was then that I woke up and set off the ship. As I drew near, the smoke swirled round me, heavy with the odour of hot, dripping fat. With a groan of horror, I cried out in protest to the heavens:

"Oh, immortal gods, why did you send sleep down on me and leave my comrades to carry out this dreadful deed?"

Meanwhile, however, Helios had learned what happened from his daughter Lampetia. Beside himself with rage, he roared:

"Almighty Zeus, and all you other gods who live on Olympus, make these impious mortals pay a heavy price for slaughtering my cattle that I loved to gaze on from the sky! If they do not receive the punishment they deserve, then I shall bury myself down in Hades, and give my light to the kingdom of the dead."

It was Zeus himself who gave the sun-god the answer he required.

"Helios, give your light to gods and men as you have always done," he reassured him. "I promise you that I will smash their ship to splinters with a thunderbolt when they are in the middle of the open sea."

How could I know what the god replied, you wonder? Well, it was Calypso who told me. She was immortal, too, and word gets round among such beings.

When I got back to my comrades I let them feel the harsh edge of my tongue – not that it served much purpose, for the harm was done by now.

Six days the doomed fools ate their way through Helios' prized oxen, although the gods sent awful portents. The flayed hides crawled along the ground, the red meat bellowed, and the noise of cattle was in our ears continually.

On the seventh day, the wind stopped blowing so we went aboard and sailed away over the sea.

The island was far astern, and there was nothing but sky and water all around, when a black cloud unfurled above our heads, darkening all the sea below it. A moment later, a raging west wind came and snapped the stays which held the mast. It toppled over, smashing the steersman's head. Poor fellow! Down into the waves his lifeless body plummeted, while his soul took flight into the heavens. Suddenly, Zeus flashed and rumbled as his thunderbolt struck at our ship and filled it with choking, sulphurous fumes. My companions were flung into the sea, where they bobbed around like crows, with no hope of being saved. The gods had brought their homeward voyage to its close. I was still on board, but the savage waves soon tore away her sides, the fallen mast broke loose, the keel parted from the ribs, and she was a ship no longer. I clung to the floating mast, and when a wave rolled us both against the keel, I got a grip on it and lashed the two hulks of timber with some rigging. Hauling myself up, I sat there at the mercy of the wild wind and waves.

Soon it stopped blowing from the west, but a south gale sprang up and drove me into graver danger still, roaring with all its might to push me back into the clutches of Scylla and Charybdis. All night it drove me astern, and when the sun came up I was right back in the dreaded straits, being blown onto Charybdis' rock at the very moment she was greedily sucking in the sea.

Summoning every ounce of strength left in me, I leapt and grabbed hold of a branch of the wild fig-tree which overhung the whirling maelstrom. The monster slurped the water down and my makeshift raft went with it, while I hung there by my fingers like a bat, waiting for her to cough it up again. It was noon before Charybdis began to spew sea up once more and I caught sight of my timbers. Letting go the bough, I dropped into the waves below. A few swift strokes and I was back on board again. Paddling with my hands, I got out of those accursed narrows with all the speed I could. As for the dreaded Scylla, Zeus must have hidden me from her eyes, or I would never have come out of there alive.

Nine days I was battered by the waves, and on the tenth I made landfall on the island of Calypso, that goddess so beautiful and so terrible who cared for me and gave me all her love. But why repeat that story? I recounted it all last night, in the palace, and who cares for a twice-told tale?"

BACK TO ITHACA

Odysseus finished, and a spellbound silence filled the shadowy hall. Alcinous was so impressed that he proposed they offer him still more gifts, and the other nobles readily agreed.

Meanwhile, the ship had been got ready. Odysseus would sail next day, at sunset. In the first light of dawn they carried the presents down to the quay, and Alcinous himself was there to see them safely stowed in the ship's hold. Soon, preparations for a farewell feast were under way. A whole ox was roasted and the marvellous blind minstrel

Demodocus was called to sing the songs they loved to hear. But Odysseus was impatient for the voyage homewards to begin, and kept looking upwards at the sun, anxious to see it set. When its bright disk was low above the horizon, they all rose and filled their cups with wine. Odysseus first gave a toast to Alcinous and wished him a long reign made happy by his people's love. Then he handed a cup to Arete, saying:

"May all be well with you, most noble queen. I wish you health, and the joy of home and family." And with these words he walked out through the door, tears shining in his eyes.

When the sun set, Odysseus went on board the ship and lay down on a mattress spread with fresh linen which the crew had put out for him. They sat down to whip the sea up with their oars, while the gods sent Odysseus into a sleep so sweet and sound he might have been a dead man.

Swifter than a stallion the Phaeacian vessel leapt across the waves. Not even the falcon could have matched her speed, and he is the fleetest of all winged creatures. Onward she sped, carrying home a man whose wisdom matched the gods', but who now slept quietly, forgetting all his troubles.

All night the ship cut through the sea, and by the time the bright morning star had risen she had already come in sight of Ithaca. They made landfall at a harbour men call Phorcys, after the Old Man of the Sea, a place where

...Odysseus was still fast asleep, so they took the mattress
by the corners and laid it gently down upon the beach...

there's a cave with two gurgling springs, and an olive tree before it. This lovely spot is sacred, and Naiads live there. In it you can see stone jars of wine and bowls where bees make honey. There are looms, too, carved from the living rock, where these water-nymphs weave cloth of sea-purple, a miracle to behold. There are two doors to the cave — one to the north, for mortals, and the other to the south. This is for the gods alone, and men may not pass in or out through it.

The Phaeacian sailors were familiar with this bay and brought their ship in with such speed that she ran up half her length upon the sand. Odysseus was still fast asleep, so they took the mattress by the corners and laid it gently down upon the beach. Next they unloaded all the gifts and piled them by his side. Once this was done, they pushed their ship back in the water, clambered aboard, bent to the oars and set off back for home.

Poseidon was angry with the Phaeacians, though. He knew Odysseus must get back some day, but these fellows had not only brought him safe and sound to Ithaca but loaded him with even more rich gifts than he would have had if he had kept his loot from Troy. And so, the moment the Phaeacians' ship got back and was pulling into harbour he transformed it into a rock, to be forever beaten by the waves. When Alcinous saw this he shook his head in sorrow and remembered the prophesy which his father had once made. He immediately called on his people to offer up rich sacrifices to the sea-god, in the hope he would take pity on them and not wall their city in with lofty mountains.

Meanwhile Odysseus had woken up but could not recognize his own homeland, for Athena had spread a thick mist over everything. She did not wish him to be seen by anyone until the suitors had been punished by death.

As for Odysseus, he was overcome with despair.

"Where have I landed now?" he groaned. "What shall I do with all these treasures if the people of this place do not respect the gods, and have no laws?"

While he was worrying over this, and lamenting the dawning of another day of exile, Athena approached, in the guise of a young shepherd.

Odysseus was delighted to see another human being, and begged the shepherd to take pity on a stranger and tell him what land this was.

"You surprise me by your question, stranger," Athena replied. "Everyone knows this place. Why, even in the farthest corners of the world, eastwards towards the rising of the sun, and west, to where it sets, you will find thousands who can tell you of it. It is a rocky land, and it has no roads for chariots or horses, but yet it is not poor. Barley and wheat grow here in abundance. The rains are plentiful and there's enough lush grass to graze great herds of goats and oxen. There are trees here of all kinds, and water gushing from the springs. Stranger, you're on the famous isle of Ithaca!" Odysseus' heart leapt in his breast, but he carefully concealed his joy. To avoid revealing his identity, he spun the shepherd this yarn:

"We heard a lot about Ithaca when we were fighting over there in Troy. The reason I am here now with these treasures is that I had to flee from Crete, where I killed Idomeneus' son Orsilochus. He tried to rob me of the booty that I won in war, but got the punishment he deserved. I made my way down to the shore, where I found a trading vessel and paid the crew a handsome fee to carry me to Pylos or to Elis. The wind was against us, though, so we put in here. We were so exhausted that we came ashore to rest. Once my head hit the sand, sleep overcame me, and the others left without waking me up — not that they touched my treasure, mind you; they only kept what I had given them."

Athena smiled to hear all this, and assuming her womanly form once more she fondly stroked his cheek and said:

"Odysseus, there's no stopping you! Even a god could not outwit you when it comes to cunning and inventiveness. However, you did not know Pallas Athena when you saw her! I have come, once more, to be of help to you, for fate still has some dangers you must overcome, this time within your very own house. That is why you must tell no one who you are, but be patient for a little longer and suffer in silence."

"I did not recognize you, goddess," Odysseus admitted, "but then, how could I, when you can take on any form you choose? I have not forgotten how you watched over me when I fought at Troy. It was a different story when the voyage home began; then I lost sight of you and ill-fortune dogged my steps. Not till I reached the land of the Phaeacians did I find you at my side once more, and now you are here beside me yet again. Tell me, I beg you, is it true that I have reached the homeland that I long for?"

"Yes, Odysseus, it is – but do not grumble that I did not help while Poseidon was pursuing you. There was nothing I could do, for the kingdom of the sea belongs to him, and after all, he is my father's brother. Yet here you are on Ithaca once more, and it was with my aid."

As she said this, she drove the mist away and said:

"Look around you. Here is Phorcys' harbour, and there is the olive tree with the cave behind it, where you used to come and sacrifice to the nymphs."

Odysseus was filled with joy to see the land of his fathers after all the troubles he had been through. Tears streaming down his cheeks, he knelt and kissed its beloved soil.

But the goddess did not let him weep for long.

"Hurry, Odysseus, we have no time to lose," she warned him. "First let us hide these treasures in the cave, where no one can lay hands on them, then we shall see what's the best thing to be done."

When the gold and other gifts were safely concealed, Athena told Odysseus about the suitors. When her tale was over, she added:

"Now it is up to you. Three years these villains have been eating you out of house and home and making your good wife's life a misery. It's time they were dispatched."

Odysseus could hardly find words to express his gratitude.

"Dear goddess," he said, "without your aid I might have met a fate like Agamemnon's when I set foot in the palace, but with you at my side they'll get what they deserve, the lot of them."

"I shall be with you, Odysseus," she answered, "but first you must be made unrecognisable, so nobody will know you have returned. That done, you must pay a call on Eumaeus, your faithful swineherd, while I make haste to find Telemachus and tell him to return. He is far away in Sparta, seeking news of you."

"Why did you let him go there, goddess?" Odysseus complained. "Was it right to let strangers sit here and bring ruin on our house while you sent the poor lad off on a fruitless search in foreign parts?"

"Don't worry about Telemachus," she reassured him. "He's having a splendid time in Sparta. Granted, the suitors are lying in ambush to kill him on the voyage back, but if they did but know it, it's their own deaths that await them."

Having said this, the goddess laid her golden sceptre on Odysseus and immediately he was transformed into a

...The dogs heard his approach and flew at him with
savage barks...

wrinkled, bald old beggar, withered by poverty and life's misfortunes. She dressed him in tattered, evil-smelling rags and giving him a stick to help him on his way, she bade farewell and set off for Sparta, while he followed her instructions and took the path which led over the hillside towards the cabin of his faithful swineherd.

It did not take him long to get there. The dogs heard his approach and flew at him with savage barks, but Eumaeus came running out and drove them off.

"That was a close thing, grandpa," he told Odysseus in relief. "They nearly got their teeth in you, and then how you'd have yelled — as if I hadn't got enough problems already, working night and day to feed a bunch of wicked idlers when my good master would be grateful for a scrap of bread in god knows what distant land — if he still lives, that is. Anyway, come in and have a bite to eat, then you can tell me who you are and how you come to be so down on your luck."

Eumaeus' kind words warmed Odysseus' heart.

"I pray that Zeus, whose eyes see all, may grant your heart's desire for giving me this friendly welcome," he replied.

"Stranger, I would not think it right to slight any passer-by Zeus sent my way, even one as down-at-heel as you — but if only it were my lost master standing in your place! He would have shown his love for me by giving me a house and land and a pretty little wife. Alas, though, he is dead and gone – and if only Helen and all her kin had died before him, so many souls have gone down to Hades on her account!"

With this bitter comment he went out to the pens and caught a pig which he slaughtered and dressed and brought in hot upon the spit when it was roasted well, sprinkling the meat with barley-meal. Then, offering Odysseus wine in a cup of ivy-wood, he said:

"Eat up, old man. I'm afraid it's only these scrawny young pigs which we slaves get to eat, while the fat boars go down to the suitors, who have no fear of god in them for the injustice that they do. Perhaps they have already learned that my lord's dead, and that's why they stay on, although they know Penelope does not want them, eating their way through the master's fortune and making merry with his serving-girls. As for me, I have no choice but to pick out the finest hogs each morning and send them to their lordships."

Having made a hearty meal, Odysseus handed Eumaeus the cup so he could drink in turn, then asked him:

"Tell me, my friend, who is this master of yours? I may have met him somewhere, for I have travelled the world and fallen in with many men."

"No, no, old man," the honest swineherd answered. "No traveller who ever brought news of my lord has yet persuaded those who love him that he really did know something. Many of those who pass this way hide the black truth and go up to the palace to tell a pack of lies just for a plate of food. There's not a beggar comes to Ithaca who hasn't been to tell his wife such fairy-tales. What can she do but take them in and ask? Yet nothing ever comes of it but tears of bitter disappointment. You, too, grandpa, you'd find it all too easy to spin the queen some yarn if you knew you'd get a cloak and tunic in return. No, my master's bones have been gnawed clean by the dogs and birds of prey, or the fish have eaten him and now his bleached skeleton lies buried in the sand upon some distant shore. Yes, that's the way he must have gone, leaving his folks with bitter troubles, and me more than all. I was but a lad when I was separated from the parents who brought me up so lovingly, but much as I long to set eyes on them again, my heart burns with an even greater wish to see Odysseus, although I feel disrespectful, calling him by his name like that, even when he's gone and cannot hear me.

"Well, friend," replied Odysseus, "call me a liar if you will, but your master's on his way. I know what I am saying. As for my gifts for bearing the good news, the cloak and tunic that you spoke of, you can give them to me when he comes, but not till you have seen him with your very own eyes; for if there's anything I hate worse than the gates of hell, it is a liar, even if poverty drives him to it. I swear upon Zeus, the meat and drink you gave me and this hearth of Odysseus where I have sought shelter, that all will come to pass just as I have declared. It will not be long before the king returns, and when he does he will deal harsh punishment to those who have scorned his wife, his fine young son, and all who love him."

"Don't hope for gifts, old man," Eumaeus answered sadly, "for my lord is never coming back, I tell you. Just drink your wine up and let's talk of other things, for it breaks my heart to think of him. No more great oaths, now – let's just say that I wish Odysseus would come back, and so do Penelope, and old Laertes, and that grand lad Telemachus. Ah, it's him I pity, for he's gone off to Sparta to learn about his father, and the suitors have laid a trap to murder him before he even gets back to Ithaca. However, tell me of your own troubles. Who are you? Where do you come from? And how do you come to be here on our island?"

Much as he wished to, Odysseus could not yet reveal the truth to the good swineherd.

"I am from the wealthy land of Crete," he answered. "When my father died, he left us a great fortune, but my brothers gave me least of all because we were not born of the same mother. Nevertheless, I married a good woman from a wealthy family. I was never a coward, and I did not run away from war. I always looked death straight in the eye and stood in the front ranks of the warriors. I loved the sea as well. Nine times I captained a crew of free souls like myself, and nine times we made a fortune. I went to Troy, too – indeed, there was no choice. Everybody went. When I got back, I did not enjoy the company of my loved ones very long. I yearned for fresh adventures and so I left for Egypt. I stayed there seven years, and had some close shaves, I can tell you! I amassed a greater fortune in those parts than I had ever made before, but in the end I was tricked by a Phoenician. He told me I could earn more gold by far if I went off with him, so I went on board his ship with all my treasure. However, I soon realized that I had fallen into a trap and he was taking me to Libya for some evil purpose. Whatever it may have been, Zeus was against it, for he sent a thunderbolt and burnt the ship. We all found ourselves floundering in the waves, but I escaped because Zeus blew the mast towards me and I clung to it. Nine days I battled against raging seas, and on the tenth I was thrown ashore in the land of the Thesprotians. The king's son found me there, and out of pity he took me to his father, Pheidon, who gave me clothes to wear and took me in. It was there at the palace that I learned of Odysseus. The king himself told me he had given him hospitality, and showed me the treasure of copper, gold and iron he had brought with him. There was enough there to feed a people for ten generations! However, I did not see Odysseus in person, as he had gone to the oracle of Dodona to learn how he might find his way back home. As for the king, he swore he had the vessel ready and waiting which would sail him back to Ithaca. I left earlier, however, aboard a ship which was to take me to Dulichion. But as soon as we were out at sea, the sailors decided to sell me into slavery. They stripped me naked, then tossed me these stinking rags which I wear now. That evening we reached Ithaca and anchored in a lonely cove. Leaving me trussed up tightly in the ship, they came ashore to eat. Straining with all the strength I had in me, I managed to snap my bonds, slide quietly down the steering-oar and swim to the safety of another beach. Next morning they came in search of me, but in vain, and so they went on board again and sailed away. When they had gone, I took the path up the hillside until I reached the cabin of a man with a kind heart. It seems that I was fated to survive."

Eumaeus believed every detail of this string of lies except the part that really was true: that his master was alive and would return.

"I'm sorry to hear what you have been through, stranger, but you shouldn't have added all those tales about my lord Odysseus," he reproached him. "I know he's met with some black fate, for if he'd died a hero's death in Troy, the Achaeans would have raised a lofty monument in his honour. But now I'm sure he's come to some inglorious end, and I don't want to see a soul. The only time I go down to the city is when Penelope sends for me because someone claims to have brought news. When that happens, they all sit down and question the newcomer closely. And while some weep for the king we lost in foreign parts, others rejoice and go on eating up his fortune without pity.

As for me, I don't believe anything any more, ever since I was tricked by that Aetolian. He told me he had seen Odysseus on Crete, patching up his ships, and that he'd be here by the summer, or autumn at the latest, loaded with booty. And you, unfortunate old man, who came here with the assistance of the gods, do not hope that you will win my heart by telling lies. That will get you nowhere. If I pity you, it is because my heart already tells me to, and so does Zeus."

To this Odysseus replied:

"I never met a fellow harder to convince! I see my words were wasted on you. Come now, let us make a deal. May the gods be our witnesses that if things turn out as I have foretold and your master does indeed return, then you will give me the cloak and tunic as a present for the news I bore, and send me on my way to Dulichion. But if Odysseus does not come back, order the slaves to cast me down from a high cliff, to serve as a dreadful warning to every scrounging liar who would swear false oaths."

"Oh, yes?" retorted Eumaeus, "and what sort of name would I earn for myself if I flung every man I fed and sheltered to his death? How could I bring myself to sacrifice to Zeus, were I to do such things? But enough of that; it's getting close to dinner-time, and any moment now my two assistants will be here."

It was not long before the herdsmen came. Eumaeus commanded them to bring a well-fattened hog and slay it for the visitor. With the others' help, he prepared the pig and roasted it, then cut it into seven portions: one for the forest nymphs, one for Hermes, the protector of herdsmen, one with the spare ribs for his master lost in foreign lands, and the other four for each of them.

Then Odysseus said: "Eumaeus, may Zeus love you as much as, I have come to do, for the honour and respect you show to your unlucky master."

When they had eaten their fill they prepared themselves for bed. Eumaeus spread some sheepskins for Odysseus by the hearth, but went off himself to sleep beneath a rock, close by the pigs. Odysseus rejoiced to see how faithfully the herdsman watched over his master's property.

While Odysseus was stretched out on the floor of Eumaeus' hut, his son Telemachus was lying in a silver-studded bed in the palace of Menelaus.

As he slumbered, the goddess Athena appeared before him in a dream and told him that the time had come to leave for home.

"Take care," she added, "for the suitors are lying in wait for you in the straits of Same. They plan to seize your ship and murder you. Do not pass that way on your return, but come ashore in some deserted part of Ithaca and let your comrades sail alone into the harbour. Stay away from the city and make for the hut of the swineherd Eumaeus, who has always had your best interests at heart. Spend the night there, and in the morning send word to your mother that you have returned and she can set her mind at rest."

And so, next day, Telemachus and Peisistratus bade farewell to Menelaus and set off on the journey home.

At the same time as Telemachus was boarding ship for the crossing to Ithaca, supper was being laid in Eumaeus' cabin, where Odysseus, who wished to put the swineherd to the test, announced:

"Listen, my friend, tomorrow morning I shall go into the city to beg. I shall call on Penelope as well, and tell her all I know about Odysseus. After that, I shall see if I can find employment with the suitors, in return for my food. I have imposed myself upon you long enough."

"Are you mad, stranger," cried the horrified Eumaeus, "throwing yourself on the mercy of those suitors when they have no shred of feeling for the poor and the unfortunate? Stay here! You are no burden to me, and when Odysseus' son comes by, he will dress you in clean clothes and send you where you want."

"My thanks, Eumaeus," Odysseus replied, "and may Zeus, who sees all, give you what your heart desires. You have saved me from a hateful bondage, for there is nothing worse than beggary. But now that you intend to keep me here I want to ask you something. Tell me, do Odysseus' mother and father still live and see the light of day?"

"The unhappy Laertes still lives on, although he begs Zeus to cut the thread of his miserable existence. Night and day he weeps for the son he lost in distant lands, and for his wife, the good Anticleia, who melted away like wax and faded into darkness with Odysseus' name upon her lips. A horrible death, to be consumed by grief and sputter out like a dying candle. I hope no others that I love will ever suffer it."

"Tell me, Eumaeus, could it have been that way your own parents lost you?" Odysseus gently asked. "Your manner of telling it put the thought into my mind."

"If you wish to hear my sorry tale, then drink your wine and listen. Incredible though it may seem to you, I am the son of Ctesius, king of Syrie, a distant isle way over to the west, where the sun sets. It is a blessed spot, where men know neither hunger nor disease, and when old age creeps on them, Apollo and Artemis grant them a death as sweet as sleep. There are two communities upon the island, but they dwell in brotherhood, for my father governs wisely. One day, however, a crew of thieving Phoenicians put into port in a ship piled high with trinkets. We had a girl from those parts living in the palace then, a tall, pretty, nimble-fingered creature, and I loved her in my childish way and was always running after her. But it was she who brought about my downfall. The lovely baubles which the traders had on board their ship quite turned her head, and she began to spend more time with her compatriots than was good for her. It ended up with her stealing three cups of solid gold out of the palace, taking me by the hand and sailing off with them. I was just a little boy, and I never realized that by going with her I would lose my father and mother for ever. Six days we sailed across the sea, and on the seventh Artemis loosed an arrow which sent the treacherous hussy toppling dead into the hold. The Phoenicians simply dragged her out and tossed her in the sea to feed the fishes, while I sat there crying fit to break my heart. Along their route, they stopped off at this island to sell me to the highest bidder. It was lucky for me that Laertes offered them the largest sum. Since then, I have put my roots down in this place."

"Your story moves me deeply, Eumaeus," Odysseus replied, "but at least Zeus found you a good master to soften the blow of your misfortune, while I am still pursued by the anger of the gods, wandering the world, a stranger in strange lands."

The hours passed in conversation, and when they fell asleep the night was nearly over.

Dawn's pearly light was gilding the horizon when Telemachus reached Ithaca. His ship slipped into a deserted cove, and the suitors lying in wait for him were unaware he had taken another route.

Telemachus jumped ashore and told the sailors:

"You sail her on to the city, while I go up to see the herdsmen. I'll come down to the palace in the evening." And with these words he set off for Eumaeus' cabin.

When he arrived, Odysseus and the swineherd were getting their breakfast ready. The other men had already gone out to graze the pigs. Hearing his footsteps, Odysseus glanced through the open doorway and saw the dogs jumping and wagging their tails.

"Eumaeus!" he called out. "There's someone coming, and he must be one of yours. I can see the dogs frisking round him, and not a bark from one of them."

As he was speaking, who should cross the threshold but his beloved son! The swineherd sprang to his feet, and in his joy the wooden cup he held slipped from his fingers. He threw himself on the young man and hugged him to his breast like a father who sees his dear and only son returning from the jaws of death.

"So you've come back, Telemachus!" Eumaeus cried in a voice choking with love and admiration, while Odysseus looked on, feeling as if his heart must burst. "You've come, my lad, and here I was telling myself I would never see you again. Come on in, and let me warm my heart with looking at you."

"With all my heart, grandpa. It was to see you that I came here, and to learn what's happening in my father's house."

"Nothing has changed. Your mother's days are spent in grieving, and her nights in bitter tears of hopeless longing for your father's return."

Saying this, he took the young man's spear and led him

in. Odysseus stood up to make room for him.

"Be seated, stranger," Telemachus checked him. "There's a man here who can find a place for me."

Odysseus sat down again and Eumaeus made a pile of green twigs, over which he spread some fleeces to make a seat for the young man. On the table he placed roast meat left over from the day before, a basket piled with bread and some wooden cups of wine. When they had toasted one another and eaten a hearty meal, Telemachus asked the swineherd:

"Tell me, grandpa, how does this stranger come to be with you?"

"He is a Cretan," Eumaeus replied. "Had some hard times and knocked about all over the world, he says. Just now, he escaped from a Thesprotian ship which was carrying him into slavery, and came to me. I put him in your hands. Take him along with you and give him whatever help you see fit."

"Eumaeus, how can I take him to the palace with those foul-mouthed suitors in control? I'd feel really guilty when they started cursing him," was Telemachus' sensible reply. "Keep him here a little longer, so I can bring a cloak and tunic, sandals and a sword for him. Afterwards I can send him wherever he wants to go – but as for leaving him to the mercies of that jealous bunch, no, never!"

"My good friends," Odysseus broke in, "it grieves my heart to hear what you are suffering from these suitors. Tell me, though, young gentleman, could it be that the people are against you, and that is why you have to give in to them? Have you fallen out with your brothers, maybe, and cannot put up a united front to fight these fellows? Ah, if my hands still had the strength to match the courage of my heart, or if I were Odysseus' son, or if I saw the man himself returning – and there is hope he will – then let one of your enemy's swords strike off my head if I wouldn't march in there and bring destruction on them all!

Telemachus answered his questions.

"Stranger, the people are not against me, and neither have I quarrelled with my brothers, since I have none. The truth is, Zeus has made my family go by ones. Arceisius had one son, Laertes. One son was born to him: Odysseus. Odysseus in his turn had one son, – I am he – and left for Troy before he could take any pleasure in me. That is why my house is now filled with enemies who cast lustful eyes upon my mother and plot to do away with me. But run off now, Eumaeus, and let her know I'm back again. She must be worried sick, and I don't wonder at it. Oh, and tell the trusty Eurycleia to get word to old Laertes with all speed possible."

The swineherd hastily buckled on his sandals and set off. Then Athena, who had been watching over Odysseus all the while, appeared before him in the doorway. Only he saw her, though, and not Telemachus, for that was how the goddess wished it. She beckoned to him from the opening, and when Odysseus came out she told him:

"Odysseus, are you ready, as always? Reveal yourself to Telemachus now and work out a plan together to destroy these suitors. I shall be at your side, I promise you."

With these words she touched him with her sceptre and turned him once more into a handsome, strong man clothed in a spotless cloak and tunic.

The goddess then disappeared from sight and Odysseus went back into the cabin. Telemachus could not believe his eyes at what he saw.

"Stranger," he cried, "you must be some god if you can change your appearance in this way. I go down on my knees before you and will offer you rich sacrifices if only you will take pity on our misfortune."

"I am no god," replied Odysseus, "but I am the one whom you have always longed to see. Your days of suffering and humiliation are over, Telemachus. It is your father who stands before you!"

Odysseus threw his arms around his son, kissing him fondly, while the tears he had held back so long ran down his cheeks in floods.

But Telemachus could not yet believe that this was no immortal.

"It happened before my very eyes," the boy protested. "No mortal man can do such things. Until just now you were a poor old man in rags, and here you are looking like

..."I am no god," replied Odysseus, "but I am the one
whom you have always longed to see...

a god – and a god you must be, not my father."

"Believe it or not, I am Odysseus. Almighty Athena worked the miracle you saw. Nothing is beyond the powers of the immortals. They can turn a man into a noble hero or a humble beggar at will."

Finally persuaded, Telemachus embraced his father and burst into sobs of joy. Odysseus could not hold his tears back either, and they shook and cried in their relief louder than sea-eagles when cruel hands snatch their new-born from the nest. At last, Telemachus asked his father how he had reached Ithaca.

"The Phaeacians brought me," Odysseus replied, "and put me ashore in a remote inlet. More of that later, though. Our task right now is to find a way of wiping out our enemies. Tell me who these fellows are and what their number is, so we may see what help we shall require."

The cautious Telemachus was horrified by his father's fighting words.

"Father, I always knew you were a swordsman second to none, with a mind keen as your blade," he answered, "but how can we take on so many of them? We are not talking about ten or twenty, you know, but many, many more. For a start, there are fifty-two from Dulichion alone, and all picked men. Twenty-four more have come from Same. There's another twenty here from Zacynthos and a dozen from Ithaca itself. If we go out to face that lot, one thing alone is sure: we'll pay a heavy price for our foolhardiness

– unless we have strong help from somewhere."

"And that we shall have," Odysseus replied. "Athena will be at our side, and Zeus too, if need be."

"If we have such helpers, father, we won't need any others," replied Telemachus.

"We shall have them," Odysseus assured him. "Now, listen to me. Early in the morning, before it's even light, you must set off for the palace. I shall come on later, with Eumaeus, but wearing my beggar's guise once more. Be careful not to show your anger if you see the suitors insulting me in my own house. Even if they kick and strike me, you must keep a hold upon yourself. Do no more than tell them not to be such fools. If they ignore you, so much the worse for them! Now, here's another thing you must remember. When you see me give the nod, take all the weapons out of the hall and hide them in the loft. If anyone asks you why you are removing them, just fob him off with some excuse like: "They're losing all their brightness down here in the smoke. Already they're far from how my father left them. Besides, I am afraid you may get drunk and start killing one another. You know the saying: "Bare blades in sight tempt men to fight". Yes, tell them that and take the things upstairs. But leave two swords, two shields and two spears handy for when we launch our attack on them. There is one other thing you must be careful of: tell no one that I have returned, not even Penelope, for in her joy she may let a word slip some-where and thus warn the suitors."

While these plans were being laid, the ship that had brought Telemachus put into harbour. The moment it had docked, a sailor ran to tell the queen they were safely back and that her son was with the herdsmen. Outside the palace he came across Eumaeus, who was also going to tell her the good news.

When they went in and saw Penelope, the seaman cried, "Your son is back, your majesty!" Eumaeus then went up to her and delivered Telemachus' message, and when the queen heard she buried her face in her hands and wept for joy. But the suitors heard the news as well, and they were far from pleased. With a black look on his face, Eurymachus told the others:

"The brat has slipped our clutches – and we took him for a good-for-nothing! Now we must send a boat over to our comrades and tell them to return."

Just as he said this, the suitors' ship hove into sight.

"It's them," Eurymachus said. "It looks as if they saw the others but were too late to stop them. Let's go down and find out."

They reached the harbour as the ship was tying up alongside the quay. Antinous was the first to jump ashore. With an angry look upon his face he said:

"Some god must have let him slip away. We posted look-outs on the headlands every day and combed the straits by night in case he tried to get through without being

..."Antinous, you are a shameless plotter!" Penelope cried.
"Why do you wish to kill Telemachus?"...

seen. For all that, he escaped from Charon. Now we must work out some other plan. If he escapes death this time, I warn you things will go against us."

However, one of the suitors, Amphinomus by name, was afraid they might bring the anger of the gods upon them and cautioned the others against taking hasty action.

"I shall not lay a finger on Telemachus unless I know the gods desire it, too," he announced. "Let them send us some sign that we are free to do away with him, and I shall be the first to pierce him with my sword."

The others reluctantly fell in with Amphinomus' decision and went back to the palace with gloomy looks upon their faces.

But their conversation had been overheard by Medon, Penelope's faithful herald, who ran and told her all that he had heard. Quivering with rage and indignation, she came down from her chamber and addressed Antinous in front of all the suitors.

"Antinous, you are a shameless plotter!" she cried. "Why do you wish to kill Telemachus? Do you forget that when the Thesprotians were hunting down your father, it was Odysseus who saved him from a certain death? And now you plan the murder of his son!"

What could Antinous say? But the smooth-tongued Eurymachus had a ready answer to her furious charges.

"Honoured Penelope, that was wisely said. But listen to me, I pray. As long as I am living, you need fear for nothing. No one will dare so much as touch a hair of your son's head, or this sword will be painted with his blood. I say this for all those present to hear, for I do not forget how Odysseus dandled me on his knee when I was a little boy, popped bits of meat into my mouth, and held the cup up to my lips so I could take a sip of the sweet wine. It is in memory of this that I hold his son Telemachus the dearest of my friends and that he need fear nothing."

But all the while the vile Eurymachus was speaking, he, too, was plotting her son's murder.

Towards evening Eumaeus set off for his cabin, where he found Telemachus and Odysseus preparing a meal together. His master was dressed in rags and unrecognisable once more, for Athena had just transformed him back into a beggar. As soon as he got in, Telemachus asked what had happened, and whether the treacherous suitors had sailed back from their attempted ambush.

"I was in a hurry and did not stay to ask," replied Eumaeus. "One of your sailors was the first to break the good news to Penelope; but while I was crossing Hermes' hill on my way back I saw a ship coming filled with spearmen carrying shields, and I think that would have been them."

On hearing this, Telemachus flashed a secret smile at Odysseus. Soon they sat down to eat, for night had fallen by now.

At day-break, Telemachus tied on his sandals, took his spear and told the swineherd:

"I'm off to the palace to show myself to my mother. Perhaps she will stop crying then. You take the stranger and lead him into town to beg, for I have troubles enough of my own, and can't take care of everyone. If he feels I've let him down, it's not my fault. I am a plain man and I say what I mean."

Odysseus played his role as convincingly as his son.

"I don't want to stay here, either," he agreed. "A poor man's better off begging round the town than in the mountains! Down there, each one will give me what he has to spare. I'm too old to stay here cleaning pig-sties."

Telemachus strode off down the hillside. When he reached the palace, he leaned his spear against a pillar and went in. His nurse Eurycleia saw him first and ran with tears of joy to greet him. The faithful serving-women came running up, too, and kissed his hands, his shoulders and his cheeks. Then Penelope came down and tearfully clasped her dear son in her arms.

"Light of my eyes, Telemachus! You're back at last," she sobbed. "I thought I would never see you again when you went off to Pylos without a word. Come, sit by me and say if you have good news of your father."

"I will tell you the whole story, mother," Telemachus replied. "When I reached Pylos, Nestor received me like a long-lost son. There was nothing he could tell me of my father, though, so he advised me to go on to Sparta and see Menelaus. He gave me a chariot with swift horses and one of his sons to be my guide. At Sparta I saw the fair Helen, too, whom the gods used to bring ruin on the Trojans and the Argives. Yet what moved me most of all was not her beauty but the way Menelaus greeted me when he learned I was Odysseus' son. It seems there was not another man in the Achaean army so loved as was my father. And here's the greatest news of all – he told me he's alive! He heard it from the ocean seer Proteus, whose words are always true. The goddess Calypso is holding him prisoner on her island. Proteus saw him there with his own eyes, weeping bitter tears and gazing out across the sea."

Penelope sighed and answered sorrowfully:

"My only wish is that he is still living, for only then can there be hope of his return. Yet I fear that all my hopes and wishes are in vain." And with these words she went up to her rooms to weep afresh.

Outside the palace, the suitors were passing their time with spear and discus throwing. When the time to eat drew near, they abandoned their games and crowded into the courtyard, where they slaughtered fat sheep, well-fed goats, prime boars and a yearling calf, all taken, as usual, from the herds of this Odysseus they dismissed as 'dead in foreign fields' but who was really coming back home at that very moment to bring destruction on them.

As Odysseus came down the hillside with Eumaeus they passed the marble fountain which Ithacus had built in the old days, and there they ran into Melantheus, who had been Odysseus' goatherd but was now the suitors' man. As soon as he set eyes on them he showed his evil character.

"Birds of a feather flock together, eh, you filthy good-for-nothings? Like goes with like, and dung on cabbages! Where are you taking this idle dog, you dirty pig-man? Off to the market-place to rub his lazy back against the door-posts and beg for scraps, the cringing bowl-licker? Why don't you give him to me instead, to clean out goat-pens and bring greenstuff for the kids? But what work would I get out of a loafer who only knows how to drag his with-ered carcass round the town and whine for bread to fill his greedy gut? I warn you, if this wrinkled flea-bag dares set foot inside the palace the suitors will give him the beating of his life, or my name's not Melantheus!"

Apparently not even words like these were enough to satisfy the treacherous goat-herd, for as he passed he gave the old beggar a savage kick in the kidneys. But Odysseus did not even flinch. He took it patiently, although he could have struck the fellow with his stick and laid him out, or lifted him above his head and smashed his body on the stones.

Eumaeus did not react so calmly. Raising his hands to the heavens, he cried:

"Nymphs of the fountain, if ever my master made burnt offerings to you, grant me this favour; may Odysseus return and beat this fellow's sneering face to pulp!"

...Yet when he smelt Odysseus near him, he wagged
his tail and lifted up his muzzle...

But the sneer was still on Melantheus' lips as he retorted:

"Listen to the cur! If ever a foreign ship puts in, I'll truss him up and take him to the harbour, to sell him off at a good profit! As for Telemachus, who loves you so, just wait and see how Apollo will help the suitors snuff him out, the same way as Odysseus!"

With this he left them and hurried to the palace, where he took his place at table opposite Eurymachus, the suitor he admired and served.

By this time, Odysseus and Eumaeus had reached the palace gates.

"Here is Odysseus' house," the swineherd told him.

"I guessed as much," said his companion. "It stands out proud from all the others. But I hear the music of a harp, and singing. They must have company in there feasting."

"Yes, it is those who are wolfing down my master's fortune. Will you go in first, or shall I? As you please – but take no notice if they call you names, and watch out no one hits you."

"It's better if you go first," replied Odysseus. "I'll follow later. Don't worry if you see them curse and strike me. I've learned to live with things like that. When you're in need, you put up with a lot to get a bite of bread."

While they were talking, a hound which was lying nearby had lifted up its head and pricked its ears. It was

Argus, the dog Odysseus had reared with his own hands but had no time to enjoy the company of before war took him off to Troy. Others had taken him to hunt wild goats and hares, but now that he was old he lay neglected in the dung outside the stables where the mules were housed, so feeble he could no longer get up on his feet. Yet when he smelt Odysseus near him, he wagged his tail and lifted up his muzzle. His long-lost master wiped away a tear, turning his face lest Eumaeus see and understand. Then he said:

"Look, Eumaeus – such a fine hound and left to rot upon the dung-heap! He looks like a hunting-dog to me."

"What memories you bring back, stranger," his companion said. "That is Argus, who was once Odysseus' hound. You should have seen him as he was, before the master left. There wasn't another dog alive who had his speed and courage, and once he smelt out game there was no way it could escape him. But now he's old and Odysseus is gone, who can be bothered to take care of him? When their lord's away, servants neglect their duties, for Zeus the thunderer robs a man of half his virtue when he falls into slavery."

Having said this, Eumaeus went into the palace while Odysseus stood looking sadly at his dog. The poor beast's head lolled sideways and it sank into death's darkness willingly, happy it had lived to see its master home at last.

Telemachus was the first to spot Eumaeus as he entered, and he beckoned him to take a seat beside him. Soon

Odysseus made his appearance, although he did not come inside but sat down on the floor beside the door. The moment Telemachus caught sight of him, he took bread from the basket and a slice of meat and told Eumaeus:

"Take these to the stranger, and tell him to go and beg some from the suitors, too. When you've got to get by, you can't be shy!"

The swineherd carried the vittles over to Odysseus and passed on Telemachus' advice.

"May Zeus shower his blessings on your fine young master," replied Odysseus in a grovelling voice. "I hope that all his dreams come true." And with every appearance of gratitude he accepted the food his son had sent to him. Then he ate, while Phemius played his harp and sang.

When Odysseus had wiped the last crumbs from his mouth, he tottered to his feet to beg around the hall. He went from guest to guest, holding out his hand as beseechingly as if he had been born to it. Many gave without question, but some asked who he was and where he came from, and it was then Melantheus the goat-herd cried:

"I saw him on the road as I was coming. Eumaeus brought him, though who knows where he picked the fellow up."

When Antinous heard this he sprang to his feet.

"Why did you bring him here, you wretched swineherd? We are burdened enough with beggars as it is, and you have to drag this filthy creature in! I suppose you don't care if they gobble up your master's food!"

"You are unjust, Antinous," Eumaeus retorted. "I know a stranger is never formally invited, unless he is a master craftsman, a doctor, a soothsayer or a brilliant singer. Men such as these are welcomed with open arms, but no one wants a poor man, and you least of all. You hate me just as much, though little I care, as long as Penelope and her handsome son are living in the palace."

"Leave him be, Eumaeus," Telemachus advised. "That's just his way. He's always had a poisonous tongue. How kind of him to speak as if he had our interests at heart!"

Stung by this, Antinous shouted:

"What are you blathering on about now, Telemachus? I suppose you think we should all hand over half our dinner, and give the parasite enough to live on for three months!"

As he said this, an ugly idea came into his head and he pulled towards him the stool he had been resting his feet upon. Meanwhile, Odysseus had been begging from each guest in turn, and now he came and stood before Antinous.

"Give me something, master," he whined. "A fine gentleman like yourself should be more generous than anybody – it's only fitting – and if you are, I'll speak of you with gratitude wherever my wanderings take me. I was a man of rank myself in days gone by. I had a splendid house, slaves by the dozen and more wealth than I could count. Yet I gave to all who were in need, for I pitied the poor man and the beggar. Look at me now, though – Zeus wiped out all my fortune and reduced me to this sorry state."

Instead of being touched by this, Antinous grew angrier still.

"What stroke of bad luck brought this nuisance to our table?" he cried out in fury. "Be off with you, you filthy wretch. Begging's all you're fit for!"

At this, Odysseus drew back and said:

"A pity you do not have a heart to match your handsome face. It's clear you wouldn't give away a pinch of salt if it were yours, since you're sitting here feasting free on others' food, and still refuse me."

"So you curse us, too, eh?" Antinous roared. "This time you won't get out of here in one piece!" And he suddenly seized the stool he had pulled up and hurled it straight at Odysseus.

It crashed into his shoulder, but he stood there steady as a rock and uttered not a word — only gave a nod which seemed to say the time for his revenge was not yet come. Then he returned to his former place upon the threshold and called out to the others:

"Hear me, you gentlemen who pay court to the noble queen. Now I've learned a thing or two in my time, and I can say that no man minds being struck when he is struggling to protect his property — but it comes hard when he is beaten for being hungry and asking for a scrap of food. If there's a god who watches over beggars, may Antinous sleep in the grave before he sleeps in any marriage-bed!"

"Eat and be silent, fellow," Antinous retorted, "or else these men will drag you out into the street and flay you!"

Telemachus heard all of this with the bitterest resentment, but for the moment he held back his tears and kept his peace.

Antinous' cruel behaviour had reached Penelope's ears as well, and she said to her women:

"May Apollo strike him with his deadly arrows, just as he struck the poor beggar with the stool."

"If our prayers are fulfilled, not one of them will see the light of day again," Eurycleia added.

"Yes, nurse," agreed Penelope. "They all hate us, but Antinous is worse than black death itself. A poor unfortunate fellow came to our house to beg a little bread, and all he got from Antinous was a stool hurled at his shoulder."

Having said this, she sent a slave-girl off to call the swineherd.

"My good Eumaeus," she said when he arrived, "go and tell the stranger that I wish to see him. I have a present for him, and want to ask if he has heard anything of Odysseus. He looks to me like a much-travelled man."

"Ah, my lady, if only the suitors would be quiet down there, how you would delight to hear his tales. I had him three days in my hut and I couldn't get my fill of them. Why, listening to him tell of his misfortunes was like sitting spellbound by a sweet-voiced singer. He knows about Odysseus, too. He told me he fought with him at

Troy — and when he was coming through Thesprotia he learned that the master's there and will be returning any day."

"Run down and tell him to come here," Penelope commanded. "I want to hear all that he knows from his own lips. As for the suitors, let them make as much noise as they please. Why should they have any cares when their own fortunes are untouched? Enough of that, however; go and call the man and tell him that if he speaks the truth to me I'll fit him out with a clean robe and tunic." Eumaeus hurried down to deliver Penelope's message but Odysseus replied:

"I'd go at once, but I'm afraid of those suitors. Their malice knows no bounds. You saw how that man hit me for no reason — and nobody came to my defence, not even Telemachus. Tell the queen to wait till evening falls and all of them have gone, then I will go and tell her everything I know."

The kind old swineherd immediately took this message back to Penelope, who accepted it as reasonable. Then he went off to find Telemachus.

"It's time for me to go back to the pen and feed the pigs," he said.

"Go, then," Telemachus replied, "but come back early in the morning, for I shall want you."

Eumaeus had just left when another beggar arrived. This

one was known all over Ithaca – a great tall gangling fellow with an ugly, cunning face and a ravenous appetite. His real name was unknown, but everybody called him Irus because he carried the suitors' messages just as Iris ran the errands of the gods. The moment Irus laid eyes on Odysseus, he bristled with anger.

"Out of the doorway, filthy wretch!" he roared, "before I drag you out by the heels. Can't you see them in there giving me the nod? I'll give you just one chance to get up of your own accord, before it comes to blows."

"Why should I leave?" Odysseus answered with a frown. "I've done no harm to you, and I won't be jealous if they give you more than me. Here, the threshold's wide enough for both of us. What difference does it make to you if they give me food as well? We're both beggars, after all, and whatever they throw us, they do it for the gods. Don't ask me for a fight, though, for once my blood is up I could break your jaw for you, old man as I am. Indeed, it might be better if I did, and then you wouldn't dare come begging round the palace any more."

Irus was infuriated by this.

"Listen how his tongue wags," he cried. "On he goes, like an old fish-wife and never stops to think one blow from me will smash him to a jelly. All right, then, you miserable old man, get on your feet and let the others see the beating you will get when you pick on a young chap like me for your opponent."

The suitors heard the quarrel and did not miss their opportunity.

"Come on and join the fun," Antinous called out. "We've never seen a ragamuffins' wrestling match before! Let's work them up to a fight before they change their minds."

They all drew round, jeering and prodding them on, and Antinous added: "I say the winner ought to get a prize. What do you say to that black pudding hanging by the hearth?"

They all agreed to this.

"Very well," Antinous declared, "the pudding for the winner – and for the loser a good kick in the rump, so that he doesn't come here begging any more."

"Listen, masters," Odysseus added cunningly, "I'm an old man, broken by misfortune, and I shouldn't be taking on a strong young chap like this. What can I do, though, when this wretched stomach of mine has set its heart on that pudding hanging by the fire? But promise me that you'll all sit tight while we are fighting, and not sneak up and hit me in the back."

The suitors agreed and Telemachus added this assurance:

"Stranger, if your heart is set on fighting you need have no fear of anyone. Deal with this fellow, and if anyone thinks he can slip in and strike you, I warn him now that he'll be sorry for it."

..."That's the end of Irus – but you can't say he didn't ask for it"...

His mind at rest, Odysseus stripped down and tied his beggar's rags around his waist, revealing his burly thighs, strong arms and the well-formed muscles of his chest and shoulders. The suitors were astonished when they saw him and murmured to one another:

"That's the end of Irus – but you can't say he didn't ask for it. Just look at the strength concealed beneath those tatters!"

When Irus heard this he began to tremble like a leaf. He tried to make a run for it but the slaves held him where he was.

It was Antinous who added the final touch to his abject terror.

"Ashamed to stand up to a poor old broken man are you, you miserable great lout? Then listen to what I have in store for you. If he makes a braver fight of it than you, I'll pack you on a ship and send you over to the bogey-man, king Echetus, and he'll slice off your nose and ears, my lad, and tear out your privates by the roots to feed them to the dogs. That's what I'll do, you skunk, or my name's not Antinous!"

When Irus heard this he was reduced to a mass of quivering jelly. They had to drag him up to face Odysseus, who was now in some doubt as to what to do with him. Of course, he could deal death with a single blow, but that might give the game away. So he let Irus strike him first. The blow landed on his shoulder and he responded with a crisp punch underneath the ear. And there the fight ended. Irus sank groaning to the ground, blood trickling from his mouth. While the suitors looked on, doubled up with laughter, Odysseus seized the fellow by the ankle and dragged him out into the courtyard. Propping his sagging body up against the wall just by the gate, he thrust a stick into his hand and said:

"Sit here and keep out dogs and pigs, you filthy lout – not poor men and beggars, or a worse fate may befall you!"

And with these words he slung his own old ragged bag over the man's shoulder and went and sat down once more on the threshold. As the laughing suitors passed him going in, they called out:

"Zeus will reward you, stranger, for ridding of us that glutton Irus. Now we'll send him off to the bogey-man. King Echetus won't take any pity on him!"

Then Antinous set the black pudding before Odysseus, while another suitor, Amphinomus, fetched two loaves and brought them to him, saying:

"Good luck, old man, and may the gods put a speedy end to all your troubles." And with these words, he handed him wine in his own cup.

"Amphinomus, you seem a fair and reasonable man," Odysseus said in answer, "and I have heard that your father, Nisus of Dulichion, was also kind and just, so let me tell you something you would do well to remember. There is no weaker creature on this earth than man. One day he is great and mighty, and the next day poor and weak. I am reduced to these dire straits because of all the injustices that I committed. I trusted too much in the power of my own mind and body – and now look how my fortunes are reversed. That is why a man must shun unjust deeds above all things. He should rejoice in the fruits of his own labour and accept the gifts of the gods with gratitude. Yet what do I see all around me here but the lawless behaviour of these suitors who consume the fortune and insult the wife of a man who, I believe, is no longer very far from home? Odysseus could be here now any day and you would do well to leave this place lest you find him in your path when the evil moment comes. For when he sets foot in his palace once again he will not bid farewell to the suitors without bloodshed."

Having said this, Odysseus sprinkled a few drops of wine as an offering to the gods then drank and returned Amphinomus his cup. The young man set off home with a troubled look upon his face. But he was not destined to escape. His fate decreed he would return and be there at the evil hour, and Athena would choose Telemachus' lance to strike him down.

All this while, Penelope had been in half a mind to go down into the great hall, but burdened as she was with grief, she could not find the heart to bathe and deck herself in all her finery. Then Athena granted her a deep, relaxing sleep to wipe away all trace of care and weariness. And as she slumbered, the goddess bathed her lovely face with heavenly balm and made her seem taller, slimmer and more fair-complexioned. Eventually she was woken by the voices of her women, and sitting up she said:

"How refreshed I feel! If only Artemis would grant me a death just like that sleep, instead of drowning in tears of longing for my husband, who was the finest man in all of Greece."

Accompanied by two slaves, Penelope went downstairs. When Odysseus saw her, his heart started to pound, but his face revealed nothing of his emotion. Penelope walked over to Telemachus.

"My child," she said, "what happened down here was unforgivable. First Antinous struck the stranger, then they set Irus onto him. Did you not consider what will happen if we allow every visitor to our house to suffer violence? Everyone will despise you!"

"You are right to be angry, mother," Telemachus replied. "I see the truth of all you say, for I am a child no longer. Yet how can I think calmly when I am surrounded by all these villains? Besides, the affair did not turn out as they would have wished. Look how the stranger proved himself a better man than Irus, and how the bully sits there with a spinning head."

Then Eurymachus approached the queen.

"Penelope, how beautiful you are today!" he cried. "If

all the noble sons of Greece could see you now, they would come running in such numbers that this palace would not hold them."

"Do not speak to me of beauty, Eurymachus. That faded on the day my husband left for Troy. Yet were he to return, the anguish that gnaws at my heart would all be smoothed away. I remember him the moment when he left, how he squeezed my hand and said: 'I fear, my love, that many Achaeans will be lost beneath the walls of Ilium, for the Trojans are brave warriors and none can match them in the arts of war. Who knows if the gods will allow me to return? So watch our son and take care of my aged father and the mother I revere, as you have always done, and when you see that the boy has grown into a man, then wait for me no longer, but find another husband'. That's what Odysseus told me, and now that time has come. Telemachus has reached manhood and one day that dreaded marriage must take place and plunge me into deeper sorrow still. If only that were all. In the old days suitors did not carry on as now. When they sought the hand of a noble lady they slew and ate the sheep and oxen from their own flocks, and brought other gifts as well – unlike all you, who make so free of another man's wealth."

That was the answer Penelope gave Eurymachus, and Odysseus, who had heard it all, was filled with love and admiration for her.

Evening was drawing on and the suitors now began to

dance and sing. As the shadows lengthened, some slave girls came, the ones who curried favour with the unwelcome guests, and laughing and joking with the men they lit the lamps and built up a great fire in the middle of the courtyard, taking turns to feed the flames with logs and keep it burning brightly as long as the merrymaking lasted.

"Why don't you go to bed now, girls," Odysseus offered, "and leave me to watch the fire? I don't mind sitting here till morning, if need be."

The slave-girls were none too pleased by this suggestion, for the last thing they wanted was to leave. One of them, Melantho, the sister of the goatherd Melantheus, even spoke rudely to him. She was afraid of no one, for Eurymachus was her sweetheart. With an insolent sneer she asked him;

"Have you lost your wits, stranger? Why don't you take yourself off to some fleapit of an inn and stop making a nuisance of yourself round here? Instead of keeping quiet and out of people's way, you have the gall to speak out in front of these fine gentlemen as if you were their equal. You may have beaten Irus, but if you get above yourself, don't be surprised if one of them breaks your skull and throws you out to lie in your own blood."

"Just watch your words, you slut. If I were to run and tell Telemachus what you've just dared to say to a poor stranger, he'd tear you limb from limb!"

Melantho and the other slaves were frightened by this

threat; and as Telemachus happened to appear at this very moment, they scurried off into the palace and left the stranger to tend the fire.

Now Eurymachus came up to taunt Odysseus.

"Why don't you come into my service, stranger?" he offered laughingly. "You can plant trees on my estates and cut stakes for the fences. In return, I'll give you all the bread you want, new clothes to wear and sandals for your feet. But what work could you do now that you've learned the easy life? All you can do is beg to fill that bottomless gut of yours."

Of course, the wise Odysseus had an answer ready for him:

"Eurymachus, I should be glad if you and I could have a match to see which of us is the better worker – say, cutting grass from dawn to dusk, without a bite to eat, in spring-time, when the days are long; or give me two oxen for the plough, and then you'd see how the heavy sods fell in the furrow, and how I ran it straight from edge to edge. Now, if Zeus stirred the flames of war, and I had a shield and two spears in my hands and a good bronze helmet on my head, you'd see that I was first among the first – and you would not scorn me then or call me glutton. You are just a bully, and the only reason you feel great and strong is because you are surrounded by these nobodies. It would be another story if Odysseus were to come. You'd be in such a panic, you'd find the gates too narrow for your flight."

..."Have you lost your wits, stranger?"...

Eurymachus went purple in the face with rage.

"I'll have your blood for that, you dog!" he roared; and snatching up a stool he hurled it at Odysseus' head. He quickly ducked and it hit the wine-steward instead. Over on his back he went, the pitcher smashed and the wine spilled on the ground.

Seeing all this, the other suitors said:

"The trouble we've had with this beggar! He doesn't deserve to get out of here alive!"

"Have you all gone mad?" shouted Telemachus. "Or is some malign spirit driving you on to still more hateful deeds?"

They all bit their lips and fell silent. Since no one had an answer for him and their evening was spoiled, they hurriedly went their separate ways. As soon as they had gone, Odysseus went up to Telemachus.

"Now they're out of the way, here's our chance to gather up all the weapons. Let's waste no time."

Telemachus immediately called Eurycleia.

"Close the doors of the women's chambers, nurse," he said, "while I put the spears and shields up in the loft. They're all black with smoke. I was only a baby when my father left, but now that I've grown up I intend to take better care of them."

"It's good to see you thinking of the house for once, my boy," she answered, "but who will hold the lamp for you, once I've shut the slave-girls in their rooms?"

"This good fellow will light the way for me," replied Telemachus. "He's been eating in our hall, and a little work won't harm him."

Odysseus sprang to his feet and the two of them carried up the helmets, shields and spears, while Athena herself lit their way for them. Telemachus could not understand where all this light was coming from.

"Don't be so surprised," Odysseus told him. "The gods are capable of anything. Take yourself off to bed now and leave me to talk things over with your mother."

As Telemachus was leaving, Penelope arrived with the old nurse.

"Eurycleia, pull a stool up for the stranger. I want to ask him about my husband and I'm curious to learn why he looks so sad and thoughtful."

The old woman hurried over with a stool. Spreading a sheepskin on it, she motioned Odysseus to be seated.

"Who are you, stranger?" Penelope asked once he was comfortable. "Where do you come from, and what family do you belong to?"

"Lovely queen," replied Odysseus, "ask me any other question that you wish, but not about my family or my homeland. It breaks my heart to think of them, and I am ashamed to trouble strangers with my griefs."

"Ah, stranger, do not call me lovely," the queen sighed. "Anxiety and loneliness have slowly robbed me of my

looks since the day my husband left for Troy. If he returned, all would be well again. Yet now I am beset with
cares and sorrows, for the palace is filled with proud and
heartless nobles who press me with their insolent demands
while they eat their way through my husband's fortune. I
keep to my chambers so as not to see them, and weep for
the good man I have lost. While they urge marriage on me,
my time is taken up with scheming how I may escape it. So
I set up a loom — it was the gods who put the thought into
my mind — and told them: 'Now Odysseus is lost, be patient
just a little longer while I weave a shroud for his sorrowing
father, old Laertes. We must have a windingsheet to wrap
him in when black death casts its shadow over him, and I
would not have the women of Ithaca reproach me that he
went down to Hades without funeral robes, for all the
countless wealth he had on earth'. That's how I kept them
at a distance: weaving the endless cloth all day and unrav-
elling it at night by lamplight. Three years I deceived them,
until a treacherous serving-girl revealed my secret, and they
broke in one night and caught me at it. Faced with their
angry threats, I had no choice but to finish the task — and
now I do not know how I shall escape them, for I have run
out of excuses. There you have it all, stranger — the sorry
story of my life. But tell me, now: what were your parents
called, and what land do you come from? — for all of us
have a mother and a father, a name, and a place where we
were born."

Then Odysseus replied:

"Since you insist on learning who I am, then I shall tell you all there is to know, although it grieves me to remember. It's a miserable existence when one's away from home as long as I have been."

Once again Odysseus was obliged by circumstance to hide the truth, for the time had not yet come to reveal himself to his dear wife.

"My homeland is the wealthy isle of Crete, with its ninety cities and its numerous tribes," he improvised. "I was born into a noble family. My name is Aethon, and my father was Deucalion, son of Minos. My elder brother, Idomeneus, went off to fight at Troy, while being the younger I had to stay behind on Crete. That is where I met Odysseus. Contrary winds brought him to our island while he was on his way to Troy. He asked to see Idomeneus, but my brother had already left, so I played the host myself and entertained him like a lord. Twelve days he and his men stayed with us, and on the thirteenth, when the wind had turned, we bid farewell to one another."

On he went, telling a thousand lies, and each one more convincing than the last. He spoke of long exile, of hardships and bitter disappointment, and as she listened, the queen dissolved in tears, for it all reminded her so much of her husband. Little did she know, poor woman, that he was sitting next to her! Yet for all the pity that he felt, Odysseus looked at her unblinking and dry-eyed, hiding his grief.

And then Penelope asked:

"Stranger, if it is true that you were host to Odysseus, tell me what clothes he wore, and then I will believe you."

"My lady, that is hard to say, for twenty years have passed since then. And yet there is much I do remember. He had a red cloak on, and I recall the golden brooch which fastened it, carved with a hound that held a fawn between its teeth. He wore a fine embroidered tunic, too, so smooth that it shone in the sunlight. The women could not take their eyes off him!"

When she heard this, Penelope shed fresh tears. She could not hold them back. But in the end she wiped her eyes and said:

"I pitied you the moment that I saw you, stranger, but from today you shall be my friend and an honoured guest within my house. The clothes he wore were just as you described. I wove them with my very own hands, and it was I who sewed the golden pin upon his cloak. Alas, what cruel fate drove him to leave for cursed Troy!"

"Honoured lady, do not let sorrow break your heart and wither up your beauty. Not that I blame you for it, for no wife who loses her dear husband can restrain her grief, and you much less, who lost a god among men. Yet dry your tears and hear the news I have to tell you: Odysseus is alive! He is in Thesprotia now and will be returning any day, loaded with treasure but without his dear companions, who were all drowned on the raging sea. Alone, he fought the waves whole days and nights, until he was cast up in the land of the Phaeacians. They honoured him as if he were a god, and showered rich gifts upon him. They were ready to give him a swift passage home, and he might have been here now, but he thought it wiser to go to Thesprotia first and on from there to the oracle at Dodona, to learn from the sacred oak of Zeus if he should come here openly or in secret. I learned all this from king Pheidon of the Thesprotians, who had offered him hospitality and was awaiting his return from Dodona while I was there. Indeed, he swore to the gods that he had a ship launched and waiting in the harbour to carry him back to Ithaca. But I left earlier, on a ship bound for Dulichion, and so I did not see Odysseus. I saw his treasures, though, and there was enough to feed his family for ten generations. So as you see, Odysseus is safe and will not be long in making his appearance. I swear to Zeus that everything will come to pass as I declare."

"If only all you say were true," the queen replied, "then I would heap so many gifts upon you, the whole world would be envious. But come, girls, bathe the stranger. Wash his feet and spread a bed for him with warm coverings, so he may sleep until dawn breaks. Tomorrow I wish him placed at table by Telemachus – and let the others resent it all they will."

"Don't trouble yourself on my account, your majesty," Odysseus replied. "I have been tossed about on the stormy seas so long I have come to hate soft couches and clean sheets. I shall sleep rough tonight, as I have done these many years. As for washing my feet, I do not care to have your slave-girls handle me – unless you have some good old woman whose life has been as hard as mine, and then I would not mind."

"Dear guest," Penelope replied, "no one as discreet and kind as you has ever come into my house before. I do indeed have such a good and sensible old woman, my unlucky husband's wet-nurse. She is a poor, feeble creature now, but she can wash your feet. Come, good Eurycleia, and bathe your... 'master' I was going to say – for you are his age, stranger, and his arms and legs must be wrinkled now like yours. A hard life leaves its mark upon a man."

"Alas, Odysseus, kind master," old Eurycleia wailed, "why did Zeus hunt you down so furiously, when you did honour to the gods, and made him such rich sacrifices? There was only one thing you desired: to grow old happily while your son turned into a fine young man. But thanks to Him, the day of your return will never come. And now who knows what foreign court the slave-girls mock him in, the fools, just like these bitches here? Their goings-on at night are enough to make one sick. No wonder you did not wish the whores to bathe you, stranger. Yet I will do it happily because I pity you for the hardships you have known. There is another reason, too: of all the many visitors who have passed through here, none has resembled Odysseus as

..."Odysseus, my child, how come I did not recognize you
before I felt your wound?"...

closely as you do, even to your voice and, yes, your legs!"

"Others have told me that, my dear," replied Odysseus. "It is true that to a discerning eye we do look very much alike."

Eurycleia then went and fetched a bowl, into which she poured cold water and then added hot, while Odysseus, who was beginning to fear by now that she might recognize him, moved his stool from the fireside and turned his body till it was in shadow. Since his youth, he had borne a scar upon his leg – and if Eurycleia spotted it, all might be lost.

She had begun to wash his feet when suddenly her groping hand detected the ridged scar. So great was her surprise that she dropped Odysseus' leg and the basin was knocked over, spilling all the water. Tears welled in the old nurse's eyes and she cupped her master's chin between her hands, while in a trembling voice she said:

"Odysseus, my child, how come I did not recognize you before I felt your wound?"

She swung round to Penelope, her eyes alight with the good news, but Athena turned the queen's gaze aside and occupied her mind with other thoughts, so that she noticed nothing, while Odysseus seized the poor old woman by the throat and muttered through clenched teeth:

"Do you want to bring about my downfall, nurse, now that I've come home at last?"

Eurycleia did not bat an eyelid. She understood immediately why her master must keep up his disguise.

"What a thing to say, my boy!" she answered. "Fear not, wild horses couldn't drag this out of me." And off she went to bring more water for his feet. When she was done, he wrapped his leg in rags to hide the scar and had just sat down beside the fire again when Penelope said:

"I am in two minds, dear guest. Should I stay here at my son's side, respecting the memory of my husband and my people's good opinion, or choose the kindest and most generous of the suitors and remarry? That thought would never cross my mind, save that my son is grown up now and sees the ruin they are bringing on us. So I must pick out one of them and take him to my father's house while there is still something left for Telemachus to inherit. I see the accursed day approaching when I must bid farewell to the palace of Odysseus. I think I might organize a contest for the suitors. My husband used to set twelve axe-heads upright in a row, then take aim with his bow and shoot an arrow straight through all the haft-holes. He never missed them once. That was the challenge I'd thought of setting them – and whoever gets his shot through all twelve axes, I'll take him for my husband and leave this lovely house whose sweet memories will always haunt my dreams."

And Odysseus replied:

"Adorable woman, put your plan into effect without delay – for I foresee that at the crucial hour Odysseus will appear, the only champion who can carry off this feat."

"Dear guest, I shall. But we have talked far into the night

and both of us need sleep. I shall go up to the bed that I have never ceased to moisten with my tears since the day my husband left. As for you, have them spread some coverings wherever you choose to lie."

Odysseus stretched out upon some sheepskins, but he tossed and turned as if he lay on burning coals, for his mind was awhirl with schemes of revenge upon the suitors. Not until Athena poured sweet sleep into his eyes did he lose consciousness.

Penelope had slept meanwhile, but in the grey light of dawn she woke up sobbing and prayed to Artemis, tears streaming down her face.

"Daughter of Zeus," she begged, "tonight I dreamed I had Odysseus at my side. I was so happy, for it seemed that he were real. Now I am awake again and grieving, take up your bow and end my life. Let me not gladden the heart of a lesser man than he!"

Soon the great day of the contest dawned. Odysseus and Telemachus rose from their beds while old Eurycleia gave her orders to the servant-girls.

"Give everything a careful sweep today. Put out the finest covers on the chairs, scrub down the tables well and wash the drinking-cups until they shine. We're throwing a feast for the competitors!"

Not long after this, Eumaeus the swineherd came down from the mountain with three piglets. He left them out to

root around for scraps, then came in and asked Odysseus
how he was faring with the suitors. Had they begun insulting him again?

"They can insult me all they like," replied Odysseus, "as
long as they pay for the ruin they have brought upon
another's house."

Then came Melantheus the goatherd, bringing some kids
down for the suitors' table. As soon as he saw Odysseus he
hurled more insults at him.

"Still hanging around here begging are you, fellow?
Clear out before we give you a good hiding. Go fill your
gut at someone else's table!"

Odysseus gave him no reply – just grimly shook his
head and brooded on revenge.

Now a third man came, Philoetius the chief herdsman,
driving in cows and goats. On seeing Odysseus he asked:

"Who is the newcomer, Eumaeus? Down on his luck he
seems, but still a man of quality, judging by his face. That's
the way it goes, though. The gods make life a misery for
wanderers, even if they're kings. Ah, cruel Zeus! You have
no pity on mankind. First you create us, then you afflict us
with all kinds of grief and hardship."

Then, grasping Odysseus by the hand, he said:

"Stranger, seeing you like this I suddenly recalled my
master, and I broke out in a cold sweat at the thought that
he might be like you, if he still lives – wandering somewhere dressed in rags. Before he left, he set me over all the

herdsmen and gave me his cows to mind. The herd has multiplied since then, but others give the orders now and I must bring in beef for those who eat so freely from the king's estate. Why, I'm in half a mind to take the law into my own hands and drive the beasts off to some other place, although his son's still here, for the way they carry on is more than any man can bear. All that stops me is the hope my master may show up again and pay them off in the coin that they deserve."

"Friend," said Odysseus, "you seem an honest fellow and no fool, so let me tell you this: I swear by Zeus, and by your unlucky master's hearth, and by the bread which I eat at his table, that you will still be here when Odysseus returns, and will see with your own eyes the downfall of the suitors."

"May Zeus grant that he does return," the herdsman growled, "and then you'll see what strength is in these arms!"

Soon the suitors came, and began to slaughter sheep and goats, fat pigs and a whole calf. When they were roasted and cut into steaming joints, the slave-girls brought them to the tables.

Telemachus carried in a stool and a small table for Odysseus and made a place for him beside the door, as they had previously agreed. Then he brought him a generous helping of tripe, together with a cup of wine.

On seeing this, Ctesippus, as evil a man as any in the

hall, stood up with a sneer and called:

"Just look, proud suitors, the stranger got an equal share with us – and quite right too. Now I've a little something of my own to add!"

And seizing a cow's foot from the plate in front of him, he hurled it straight at Odysseus' head. He ducked in time and stared back with a bitter smile upon his lips. It was a smile that boded ill for Ctesippus, but how was he to know? As for Telemachus, he stood up and with a stern air of confidence that left the other suitors open-mouthed, announced:

"Lucky for you the stranger dodged in time, Ctesippus, or your father would be preparing for a funeral now and not a marriage!"

Not knowing what to say, the suitors gave a few half-hearted jeers at this then threw themselves upon the food, downing one cup of wine upon the other, until their eyes were red and streaming. In their drunken madness, they seemed to be weeping at the fate which would befall them.

Then Theoclymenus, a seer who had come back from Pylos with Telemachus, called out:

"Miserable wretches! What horror hangs above your heads! What darkness veils your eyes! See how the tears are streaming down your cheeks! The time of lamentation has begun! The walls drip blood! Shades of the dead are scurrying this way and that! The sun is lost! A pall of darkness hides the sky! Black death is upon us!"

Eurymachus jumped to his feet.

"This fellow's lost his wits," he sneered. "Why don't we take him out into the sun, if he finds it dark as night in here!"

"My eyes see all too clearly, Eurymachus, and do not imagine that my wits have turned. I shall stay here no longer with you fools who have spread your feast inside the lion's den and mock those who give you a fair warning."

With these words he left the hall and made his way down to the city. As he was leaving, one of the suitors called:

"Here's a fine pair of guests you're landed with, Telemachus! One eats and drinks as if his belly were a bottomless pit and is good for neither work nor war, the idler, while the other just stands up and plays the prophet! Take my advice: truss them both up and send them over the sea to the Sicilians. They'll give enough for them as slaves to make your fortune!"

The man might just as well have remained silent for all the attention that Telemachus paid. His thoughts and eyes were fixed upon his father, anxiously waiting for the sign that would send him running to his side. All this while, the unsuspecting suitors wolfed down their lordly fare with shouts and roars of laughter. But the next course was to be the deadliest ever served. The goddess and her beggar-warrior were ready.

THE SUITORS COME TO AN EVIL END

Then Athena put it into Penelope's mind to bring the bow and axe-heads to begin the contest which would prove the beginning of the end for all the suitors.

Up the staircase she went, in all her majesty, and with a fine-wrought key opened the door of the chamber where the king's treasures were all locked away. Among them were his bow and a quiver full of arrows.

This bow had once belonged to Eurytus, the famous archer, who had outshot all the bowmen in the land of Greece, only to be defeated when he pitted his skills against

Heracles. Upon his death, it came into the hands of his son
Iphitus. Odysseus had once gone to the Peloponnese and
met with Iphitus. A bond of friendship had grown up
between them, and as a token of their brotherly love they
had exchanged their weapons. Odysseus had handed over
his sword and spear and he his famous bow. Odysseus had
kept the bow in memory of his friend and not taken it to
Troy with him. Twenty years it had lain hidden with his
other treasures in the palace, and now at last it was being
taken from its hiding-place to wreak destruction on the
suitors.

Taking it in her hands, Penelope sat down and let the
weapon rest upon her knee. Tears trickled down her cheeks
as old memories came back to her. Then she rose and
wiped her eyes and went down, bow in hand, into the hall
where she announced:

"Hear me, all you who eat and drink away the fortune of
a host who's lost in foreign lands, all you who claim you
want me for your wife, when living well at other folks'
expense attracts you more. Come now, and prove your-
selves with Odysseus' bow. If any one of you can bend and
string it, then shoot an arrow through the haft-holes of
twelve axe-heads standing in a row, I promise I will take
him for my husband and bid farewell to this lovely house I
shall remember fondly, even in my dreams."

Then she told the swineherd Eumaeus to set the bow and
the twelve axe-heads before the suitors.

Tears in his eyes, he placed them on a table, together with a quiver full of arrows. And when Philoetius saw his master's marvellous bow, he wept as well.

Antinous noticed this and cried out angrily:

"What are you snivelling for, you wretches? Either get out or shut your mouths and stop your crying. We others have a difficult contest ahead of us. It will be no easy task to bend a bow like this, for there is not a man among us who is like Odysseus as I last remember him, when he set off for Troy, and I, a child then, gazed at him so admiringly."

Flattering words — but in his heart he was sure that he could string the bow and send the arrow humming through the haft-holes.

"Enough of speeches," declared Telemachus. "Come and admire the prize: a woman whose match cannot be found in all the land of Greece. Yet why should I commend her when you know her qualities so well? Let us get started, then! All that I ask is that I be the first to try my father's bow. If I can bend it to the string and pass an arrow through the axes, I shall raise no objection to my mother marrying again. I shall stay here happy in the knowledge that at last I am fit to bear my father's weapons."

Having given this assurance, he next set up the axe-heads in a perfectly straight line. The suitors were surprised to see how well and confidently he carried out the task, for all his inexperience. Then, picking up the bow, he leant against the door-post and tried to get the string into the notch. Three times he strained to bend the bow-end to the loop, and three times he failed. On his fourth attempt he had actually begun to slip it over when he caught a glance of warning from his father and released the string.

"Must I be a weakling all my life?" he exclaimed, pretending to be angry with himself. "Why don't you suitors try instead, since you've more muscles in your arms than me." And leaving the unstrung bow against the door-jamb he went back to his place.

"Let us begin in the order we are sitting," Antinous proposed.

The first to rise was Liodes – but he was a better seer than a bowman and put it down after the first attempt.

"Let the next man try," he muttered. "This bow will cut off many in the flower of their youth, and I'll not be the one to string it."

"Come now, Liodes," Antinous cried mockingly. "You cannot bend it, so you warn us all of death? Here, Melantheus – bring us a lump of tallow, so we can grease the bow and make it bend more easily."

They heated up the fat and rubbed it deep into the dry old wood. Suitor after suitor took his turn but not one of them had anything approaching the strength which was required. However, the strongest contenders, Eurymachus and Antinous, had not yet had a try.

Meanwhile, the two herdsmen, Eumaeus and Philoetius,

had gone out into the courtyard, where Odysseus now approached them.

"I want to ask you something," he confided, "and yet I hesitate, although I don't know why. Tell me, comrades. If Odysseus were to turn up unexpectedly, whose side would you be on – his, or the suitors'?"

Both answered in a flash that they begged the gods to bring their master back, and swore by all they held most sacred that they would be there at his side.

This spontaneous demonstration of their faithfulness and courage was all Odysseus needed to convince him. Bending to their ear, he said in a low voice:

"Well, here I am – back home again! Yes, I am he, Odysseus, returned to Ithaca after twenty years of desperate adventures. Of all my men, you have shown your love most clearly. I saw it from the very first instant, and I see it now. To prove to you beyond all doubt I am indeed Odysseus, here is the scar where I was gored by the wild boar on Parnassus."

As he spoke, he unwound the strip of rag that bound his leg, and the moment they saw it and were persuaded that their master had come back they threw themselves into his arms and wept with joy. Odysseus gently cut them short and said:

"Listen – go back inside now, but one by one and not too obviously. At some stage in the contest I shall ask to try the bow myself, and if they start protesting, you run and bring it to me, Eumaeus. The moment you have done so, tell the slave-girls to leave and bar the doors behind them. If they hear groans and the clash of arms, they are not to show their faces but just get on with their work. And you, Philoetius, shut the yard door fast and secure it with a length of rope."

After giving these instructions he went back into the hall and sat down on his stool again. Soon the two herdsmen came in, one by one.

Eurymachus now had the bow between his hands. He was holding it over the fire to try to make the wood more springy. When he had heated every inch of it he tried to bend it back and notch the string, but though he strained until his face was scarlet, his efforts were in vain. Eventually he threw it down and said disgustedly:

"I am furious at myself and all of us, not so much because this puts paid to the marriage – Ithaca and the neighbouring islands are full of pretty women, after all – but because we've made fools of ourselves and shown how far below Odysseus we are. It will be generations before this humiliation is forgotten."

"Don't worry about it, Eurymachus," Antinous replied. "This is no day for stringing bows, that's all. Toss it in the corner and have the servers fill our cups. And tomorrow, when we have slain some goats and offered them to Apollo, the finest archer of them all, we shall try to bring the contest to an end."

Antinous' proposal met with general approval. Wine was brought in, the cups were filled, and when all had poured their drops out to the gods and drunk deep, Odysseus got up from his seat beside the door and said:

"Hear me, my lords, contenders for the noble queen, Eurymachus and Antinous above all. May they be right in hoping that Apollo will award the victory to the man he chooses. Meanwhile, let me try the bow as well. I only want to see if my hands have kept their grip, or whether the years of voyaging and hardships have robbed me of my former strength."

The suitors were furious when they heard this, and Antinous jumped up with a shout.

"Have you gone mad, old vagabond?" he cried. "Is it not enough that you sit here feasting with your betters and overhear our secrets? Have you drunk so much you no longer know what's good for you? Have you forgotten what happened to Eurytion the centaur when the wine went to his head and he tried to ravish women in the palace of Peirithous? Do you want your ears and nose cropped, too, if by any chance you string the bow? Or would you rather have us send you off to pitiless king Echetus, from whose clutches none can rescue you? Hold your peace and drink. Don't try to take on better men than you."

At this Penelope intervened indignantly.

"Antinous, you have no right to behave so discourteously to any guest of Telemachus – unless you fear that if the stranger bends the bow he will take me for his wife as well. He has no hope of either, I assure you. So give him the bow and do not let that prospect weigh upon your dinner."

"Noble lady," Eurymachus replied, "we do not fear this ragged stranger will take you as his bride; he is obviously too far beneath you. Yet what if the ragamuffin draws the bow and gets his arrow through the axe-heads? What will the world say then? Could there be a greater shame for us than to be beaten by a wretched beggar?"

"Eurymachus," replied Penelope, "all of you have battened shamelessly upon a brave man's house, eaten and drunk away the fortune of an absent host, so why feel shame at what the world may say if the stranger happens to defeat you? Let him try, I say. He seems a sturdy fellow, and claims he was a man of substance once himself. I only hope he pulls it off, and if he does then I shall give him a fine-spun robe and tunic, a sword and pointed spear, then send him wherever he may wish to go."

"Mother," broke in Telemachus, "it is up to me to tell the stranger whether he should try to string the bow or not, or even to let him have it as a gift if I so please, and no one has the right to try and stop me. So you go back into your quarters and mind the women and leave me to decide what's to be done about the bow or any other question that arises, since I'm the master in this house."

Pleased by the way her son had now assumed command,

Penelope went up willingly to her chambers where Athena cast a sweet sleep on her eyes.

Then Eumaeus picked up the bow to take it to Odysseus. The moment he laid hands on it an angry muttering broke out among the suitors and an arrogant youth called out:

"Where are you taking that, you dirty slave? We'll throw you to the dogs if you don't watch out — and off you'll go to Hades without a penny for the ferryman!"

At this the rest began to curse him just as loud, and in his fear he dropped the bow again. All he achieved by this was to bring Telemachus' angry shouts down on him from across the room.

"Take him the bow, old man! Don't listen to them or I'll send you scurrying in a shower of stones! I may be younger than you are, but I'm certainly far stronger. If only I had the strength to match these suitors, though, they wouldn't be able to get out fast enough!"

So Eumaeus picked the bow up once again and went and placed it in Odysseus' hands. Then he ran to find Eurycleia.

"Orders from Telemachus," he told her. "You and all the slave-girls are to bar the doors and stay locked up inside. If you hear groans or other noises, don't come peeking in. Just keep your minds upon your work."

She hastened to obey. At the same time Philoetius went to close the yard gate. Having made it fast with a length of stout ship's rope he went back to his place and waited to see what Odysseus would do next.

There he stood, examining his bow, turning it this way and that to see if woodworm had got to it. One of the suitors murmured to his neighbour:

"The fellow must have been a hunter, for he seems to know a good bow when he sees one. Perhaps he had others like it back at home. Who knows, though – maybe he's just turning it round and eyeing it so carefully because he wants to make one just the same, the sly old buzzard."

"Just wait and see what's coming to him when he puts it down unstrung," another suitor added.

But Odysseus grasped the bow, and as easily as a singer fits a new string to his harp and winds it round the peg, so

he deftly stretched the bowstring and slipped the noose into its notch, then brushed his hand across to test the tautness, making it sing as sweetly as a swallow.

The suitors paled with fear, and at that very moment Zeus loosed a clap of thunder. Delighted by this signal from the god, Odysseus picked up an arrow that was lying loose upon the table and left the ones the suitors would soon be feeling in their bodies ranged neatly in their quiver. Then he grasped string and arrow in one hand and the leather-bound grip in the other, pulled hard and true and sent the bronze-tipped missile winging through the hole in the first axe-head and straight out of the last. The feat accomplished, he turned round to his son and said:

"You see, Telemachus? Your guest has not put you to shame. I strung the bow with ease and hit the mark. I have some strength and skill left yet, however much they may despise me. What if they do? Let them eat first, then they can have as much sport as they want."

But as he spoke he lowered his eyes and nodded. And Telemachus swiftly slung his keen sword over his shoulder, took a firm grip on his sharp-tipped spear and, gleaming in his polished armour, went to join his father.

Now the great hero flung his rags aside and leapt up on the door-sill, clutching his bow and the quiver full of arrows. Spilling them out before his feet, he notched one in the bow-string, saying:

"Now let's try a target I'll be glad to hit!" And quick as lightning he took aim and loosed a deadly shot at Antinous which caught him in the throat. He was in the act of lifting a lovely gold cup to his lips, and death had been the last thing he expected. Indeed, which of them did? What man alone, no matter how courageous, would dare to strike Antinous down in front of all his friends?

In his death-throes he overturned the table. The cup he held jerked from his hand, splashing the fallen bread and meat with wine. The suitors scrambled to their feet with shouts and ran in search of weapons – but the walls were bare and neither spears nor shields were anywhere to be seen. Wild with rage, they started to hurl curses at Odysseus.

"Villain, how could you shoot towards a man?" they cried. "That's the last arrow leaves your bow, you monstrous fool – for now you've killed the finest lord in Ithaca, and your end has come!"

They said this, thinking he had loosed the arrow by mistake. It had not even crossed their minds that a trap had closed upon them. But when they heard Odysseus' voice they froze in horror.

"So, dogs, you said that I would not return! You ate me out of house and home! Seduced my serving-girls without a trace of shame! And even tried to rob me of my faithful wife! You never thought, you fools, that someday the hour would come for you to pay for these outrages with your lives!"

The suitors stood there trembling at the knees, until Eurymachus plucked up the courage to say:

"If you are indeed Odysseus, you were quite right to vent your wrath on them for all the evil they have done you. But look! The one who is to blame for all lies dead, and justly so. It was Antinous who decided everything on his own – not that he felt a pressing need to marry, but because he wished to reign in Ithaca once he had killed your son. Now he has paid the price that he deserved. As for the rest of us, we'll gather from the people all we ate and drank and give it back to you. On top of that, each one

will pay a fine of twenty oxen, as well as all the gold and copper you demand. Take all these, but do not loose your anger on us."

Odysseus glared down at him and replied between clenched teeth:

"Eurymachus, even if you gave back everything I've lost, then added all your wealth and doubled it, you still would not escape your death."

The suitors' faces turned as pale as wax at this.

"Lads," cried Eurymachus, "he'll not rest quiet until he's done for every one of us! Fight like men, I say! Pick up your knives and use the tables for shields and we'll throw

ourselves upon him all together till he's forced to leave the
doorway. After that we'll run to raise the people up – and
then it will be he who faces death, not us."

Seizing a knife, he lunged forward shouting fiercely. He
did not get very far. Odysseus' deadly arrow plunged deep
into his breast. Eurymachus, second in rank among the
suitors, was no more.

Amphinomus came hard behind him, clutching a keen
blade, but Telemachus was there in time and felled him
with his spear before leaping to his father's side.

"I'll run upstairs and bring down all the weapons that we
need," he cried. "Eumaeus and Philoetius need arming,

too."

While he went off for spears, shields and helmets, Odysseus kept up his deadly hail of arrows, and not one shot went astray. When the last had gone, he dropped the bow and snatched up a good stout shield and helmet. Jamming this on, he stooped to choose two spears and then resumed his merciless attack upon the suitors.

However, the evil Melantheus had made his way upstairs unseen by anyone, and brought down shields and weapons for the suitors.

Odysseus' heart sank when he saw them being armed.

"Who brought these weapons down, Telemachus?" he cried. "Was it some slave-girl, or Melantheus?"

"It's my fault, father, for leaving the door open. Eumaeus, run and close it!"

Eumaeus rushed upstairs where he saw Melantheus going for more swords. He shouted for assistance and was joined by Philoetius. Both men fell upon their victim, caught him and hanged him from a roof-beam in a trice. They hurried back to join Odysseus, and now the four of them, their blood at boiling point, wreaked havoc on the suitors.

Not many were left alive by now, but Agelaus spurred the survivors on. They flung their spears in a single volley at Odysseus. Athena, though, was watching over him and turned their shots aside.

"Now it's our turn!" Odysseus cried, and the four hurled

their lances in one throw. Each one found its victim. The suitors launched their spears again, but missed a second time. Once more the four companions aimed their weapons, and again each hit its mark. Philoetius had special reason to be pleased. His spear had struck Ctesippus and he called out mockingly:

"There, Ctesippus! That's for the cow's foot you threw at my noble master when he came begging in his own hall!"

Soon there was not a single suitor left alive. Odysseus now sent Telemachus to call Eurycleia. When she arrived and saw the suitors lying dead, with her king pacing like a lion among them, she could have cried aloud for joy. But Odysseus restrained her, saying:

"Nurse, keep your feelings to yourself. It is not right to triumph over the dead. It was their fate that brought these fellows low – that and their evil deeds. Just summon the slave-girls who have brought dishonour on my house. Tell them to carry off the corpses, then swill out the hall and wash the benches down. I want this place cleaned up!"

Of the fifty women serving in Odysseus' palace, twelve had lost all sense of shame and let the suitors have their way with them, treating Penelope and the older slaves with insolence. These were the ones Eurycleia now summoned. When they arrived and saw their protectors sprawled lifeless on the floor, they wailed and tore their hair, but had no choice other than to carry out the nurse's orders. When they had put the hall to rights, Telemachus instructed the two herdsmen to take them off and lock them in the cellar to await the punishment that they deserved.

"Now I shall run to wake Penelope and bring her down to you," Eurycleia told Odysseus.

"Not yet. Bring fire and brimstone first. I want to cleanse my house of all its evil memories."

The nurse obediently brought fire and sulphur, and with their purifying fumes he drove the stench of blood from hall and courtyard. When his task was finished the faithful ones among his servants came with lamps. They greeted him with tears of joy, kissing his head and shoulders and pressing his hands warmly. Odysseus was deeply moved by their spontaneous show of love, but he hid his tears, for he was ashamed to let them see him weeping.

Now Eurycleia went and woke Penelope.

"Arise, my lady! I bring you happy news. He whose return you have longed for all these years has come. Odysseus is here – and all those who made our lives a misery now lie dead!"

"Dear nurse, the gods have made you mad!" the queen replied. "Why do you mock my pain? I had not slept so soundly since my dear one left – and now you come and wake me? If any other slave had done this to me I would have sent her on her way in tears, but you I cannot scold."

"I am not making all this up, my child. Odysseus has

come, I tell you. Who could have guessed that it was he, so well he played the luckless beggar! Telemachus knew, but kept the secret hidden until the suitors paid for all the wrong they've done us."

Penelope jumped up from her bed.

"Is it true, then, nurse?" she cried. "But how could he have taken on so many? It's almost unbelievable!"

"I don't know how he carried it off, either. Nor did I see, although I heard the cries and groans while the fight was going on. All of us heard them, but we kept behind barred doors until the trouble was all over and Telemachus sent for me. And then I saw a sight beyond belief. Ah, how your heart would have swelled with pride and joy if you had seen him as I did, standing there like a lion all stained with blood, with the lifeless corpses of the suitors at his feet! But everything has been washed clean now and put back in its place, so run to greet him and enjoy the hour of your greatest happiness together, after so many years of pain and disappointment."

"Ah, nurse, I still cannot believe it. Some god must have slain the unjust suitors for all their deceitful, evil deeds — for my Odysseus, alas, was lost in distant lands."

"My good and noble lady, how can you speak such words at the very moment when I tell you that your husband is standing here below? Is it so hard for you to believe? Listen to this, then: I recognized him as I bathed his feet, for my fingers felt the wound upon his thigh. I was about to let out a great cry of joy, but he put his hand over my mouth in time."

"My dear Eurycleia, the gods work in mysterious ways, and it is hard for us mere mortals to understand their deeds. Let us go down to Telemachus, however, that I may see the dead and learn if it was god or mortal who took their lives from them."

With these words she moved towards the stairs, in a turmoil of misgivings and wild doubts. Descending to the hall, she walked across but stopped before she reached him. He sat there with bowed head, longing for a word from his dear wife. Yet Penelope stood silent, torn between her urge to rush into his arms and her doubts as to his true identity, so much had he changed.

Telemachus could not contain his anger.

"Mother, do you have a heart of stone?" he cried. "How can you stand so coldly in your husband's presence, after all he has been through? Twenty years of peril and hardship he's endured, and now he's home at last!"

"I am so confused, my child, I cannot even look him in the face," she stammered. "But if he is indeed Odysseus it will not be hard for us to know each other – for there are secrets only we two share."

Odysseus smiled at these words.

"Leave her to sound me out, Telemachus," he said. "She'll know me well enough when the time comes. Besides, the way she sees me now, dirty and wrapped in rags, it's not surprising she is not convinced. So leave her, I say, and listen to something else I have to tell you. We have killed the sons of half the noble houses in the land. When their people learn of this they'll come here for revenge and we'll find ourselves faced with a much harder battle. The longer it takes for news of this day's slaughter to get out, the better it will be. So all of you put on your finest robes, have the slave-girls deck themselves in trinkets and wear flowers in their hair, and tell the minstrel to strike up a cheerful melody that can be heard outside, so everyone will think that we are celebrating and give us time to work out our next move."

They all bathed and dressed in festive clothes, and then began to dance and sing out loud. Sure enough, beyond the palace walls the word soon spread that a wedding was being celebrated inside. The queen had made her choice at last, it seemed, and was even now marrying one of the suitors. Not a soul suspected that Odysseus had returned and killed them all without anybody getting wind of it.

Meanwhile Odysseus had bathed, rubbed oil into his body and slipped into the handsome tunic the housekeeper held ready. Athena, too, was watching over him as always. She poured immortal grace into his veins, making him taller, stronger and more handsome than before. Thus changed, he returned and took his former seat before his wife and said:

"Blind fool! You have the hardest heart of any woman I

have known. Who else could keep her husband at a distance thus, after twenty dreadful years without a sight of him? Ah well, spread me a rug to sleep on somewhere, nurse, since she prefers to keep her feelings to herself."

"Strange man," replied Penelope, "I am not as cold and proud as you imagine. It is simply that I still can't recognize you, when I think back on how you were when you went off to war. But come, my good Eurycleia, if sleep is what he wants, prepare the bed that stands outside the chamber in the courtyard, the one he made with his own hands. Spread embroidered sheets and a woollen blanket on the mattress."

But the words she spoke were only to try out her husband – and they had the effect that she had hoped for.

"Wife, you have wounded me by what you said," he answered. "How did our bed end up outside our chamber? Who could have moved it from its place, when even a god could not have moved the frame, the way that I had built it? Is that the secret which you spoke of? If so, then listen. Within a courtyard grew an olive tree with a great, thick, knotted trunk. I built four walls of chiselled stone around it, making a room with fine doors and a good strong roof above. Then I cut off the bushy branches of the tree and chipped away at its rooted trunk till I had levelled it off on top and all around to make the bed. Last of all I fitted it with carved legs and ornaments of gold and silver. That's how I made it, and that's all the proof you need to be

convinced. But how am I to be convinced that you found a
man to root a bed like that up from its place?"

Penelope was convulsed with joy when she heard Odysseus' words. Blinded by tears, she ran to him and threw her
white arms round his neck, clasping him tight and shower-
ing his face with kisses.

"Do not be angry with me, husband," she implored.
"The gods were always jealous of our love, and they have
heaped so many disappointments on us that I feared to
show my joy when first I saw you. Dear man, my spirit
trembled at the thought that it might be a trick, for there
have been so many who have wished me ill. But you have
told me all the secrets which only we two shared – we and
our faithful servant Actoris who kept guard at the door.
You have convinced me, and my hard heart is softened."

All this while she was clinging to his neck. And he
would not release her either, but hugged her fast as they
wept together with a joy that no words can describe. Dawn
would have found them weeping still had Athena not felt
compassion for them and stretched out one night into two.

"Yes, I am back, my dear," Odysseus said, "though it
has been a long and bitter wait for both of us. Our troubles
are not over yet, however. There is more to come, or so the
spirit of Teiresias told me. No more of that, though. Let us
go to our bed and enjoy a long, sweet sleep."

"The bed is ready, husband, and we can go there the
moment that you wish. But tell me first, what hardships did

the seer Teiresias tell you of?"

"Why trouble your head with them?" replied Odysseus. "Yet I will tell you, since you ask: I must go journeying to distant lands. It is Poseidon who demands this, for his anger against me is not abated yet. I must carry an oar upon my shoulder and travel on until I find myself among folks who have never seen the sea, have never tasted salted meat, know nothing of ships and do not even recognize the oars which give them wings. Listen by what sure sign I shall know my wanderings are over, though: when a passer-by stops me on the road and asks if what is on my shoulder is a winnowing-fan, then I must plant the oar upright in the earth and offer sacrifice to Poseidon: a ram, a bull and a male boar. After that I am to come back home and make splendid sacrifices to all the gods in turn, beginning first with Zeus. Then my troubles will be over and I shall reign happily in my own kingdom, loved by my prosperous and contented people. And when death steals on me at last, it will come swiftly, from the sea, in the depths of my old age. Such is the noble end the seer foretold for me."

To which Penelope added:

"Happy the man who ends a long life tranquilly, whatever trials he has endured upon his journey."

On and on they talked through that long night. Penelope told him of the miserable and anxious years she had longed for his return, while Odysseus recounted his hair-raising adventures and all the bitter experiences of the weary exile which had preceded his return.

Next morning, Odysseus, Telemachus and the two herdsmen set off for Laertes' home upon the mountainside. Odysseus was eager to see his old father once again, but he had another reason for wanting to go up there. He knew it would not be long before the slaughter in the palace was discovered and the suitors' relatives roused up the people. He could fight them better from high ground, and there he might find helpers, too.

Laertes' house was a simple farmer's cottage. The unhappy old man led a hard life there, working his fields with his own hands and with only an aged crone from Sicily to care for him. With them there lived a faithful slave, old Dolius, together with his six sons. All of them helped Laertes around the farm and their company helped to soften the pain he felt at the loss of his son Odysseus and the depredations of the suitors.

When the four arrived, they found the old woman alone in the cabin. Odysseus left Telemachus and the two shepherds there to prepare the noonday meal and went off alone to find his father. He came across him hoeing round a sapling in a well-tended garden-plot. He was wearing the clothes of a poor man, roughly-stitched and dirty. His shins were wrapped in ox-hide gaiters to protect him from the brambles and his head was covered by a goatskin hood. Odysseus' heart sank to see his father thus, and tears sprang to his eyes. His first instinct was to run and throw his arms around the bowed old figure, but then he decided it would be better to see first if Laertes recognized him. So going up to him he said:

"Old man, I see you have a well-kept garden here. No weeds around your trees – they're doing fine. But if you will forgive my boldness, I cannot say the same for you. There's no one to look after you in your old age, it seems. Your clothes are rough and soiled and your face is lined with suffering – and yet if one looks closer there is something noble in your bearing. Perhaps your master has neglected you, since he knows you will work well and faithfully whether he takes care of you or not. But tell me, is this island I have landed on called Ithaca? I did ask someone as I made my way up here, but I couldn't get any sense out of the fellow. You see, I once gave hospitality to a quite outstanding man – in fact, I've never met another like him in my life. He told me that he came from Ithaca and was Laertes' son. When he left my house, I gave him precious gifts and a golden cup to make libations to the gods, in memory of me. That was years ago, but if this is indeed the isle of Ithaca it would please me greatly to renew our old acquaintance – provided that he came home safely, that is, and still lives and prospers."

Tears rolled down old Laertes' cheeks when he heard about his son.

"Stranger, this is the place you ask of," he replied, "but

evil, grasping men now hold sway here. The gifts you gave
your friend are lost along with him. If he were here, you
could make free of his house, and as the custom is he
would offer you lovely presents in return for those you
were the first to offer. But he died unburied in some distant
land where neither the mother who gave him birth nor his
unlucky father could weep over him, nor even his patient
wife close his eyelids, as befits the dead."

And with these words he dug his hands into the dust and
scattered it on his white head with a despairing groan.

It tore Odysseus' heart to see his father's grief. Throwing his arms around him, he kissed him and cried out:

"Father, I am the son you longed to see again! It has
been twenty dreadful years, but now everything has
changed – for I have killed the lawless suitors in the palace
where they sat."

Such happiness was more than old Laertes dared to hope
for.

"If you are he, show me some sign that I may know you
by," he answered.

"Look," said Odysseus. "Here is my wound from the
wild boar on Parnassus. And wait! Let me count up the
trees you gave me here. There were twelve pear-trees, and
together with the fig-trees that made forty. Then there were
twelve others – apple-trees, I think – and then, yes, fifty
rows of vines were mine, you said, with grapes of all
varieties."

Laertes felt his knees give way with joy, and his poor heart fluttered like a bird within his breast as his son counted off these final proofs of his identity. Odysseus caught his fainting body and clutched him to his chest with longing. And even when he had recovered, he held him just as tightly as he led him to the cabin where the meal Telemachus had prepared awaited them. They arrived there just as Dolius came up with his sons. Tears streaming down his cheeks, he clapped his arms around Odysseus and kissed him, and then they all sat down to table.

Meanwhile, the slaughter of the suitors had become known in the city. Their families all gathered weeping in the square, where they were soon joined by the common people. Antinous' father, Eupeithes, rose to address them, saying:

"People of Ithaca! This man has been the ruin of our island. He took off with all our army and he lost them to a man. Of all the swift ships that he sailed away with, not a single one returned. The only one who has come back is he – and would he never had! For the moment that he found his way back here, he did us even greater harm – he murdered the sons of all the noblest families on Ithaca and the surrounding islands! You can have no doubt as to where our duty lies: we must fall on him before he gets away to Pylos or to Elis. I would rather die than live with the shame that we let our children's slaughterer slip through our fingers. Make haste! If we delay, he may have time to make good his escape."

They heard him out with sympathy; but then the seer Alitherses rose and said;

"Listen, brothers! It is the suitors themselves who are to blame for what befell them, and their fathers even more. In vain, Mentor and I advised their families to rein them in, and not leave them to their riotous wasting of a brave man's fortune and their scandalous advances to his wife. But did they listen to us? No! They thought Odysseus would never return, and carried on more wildly than before. They dug their own graves! So listen to me, all of you: off to your homes and go about your business!"

Most of the assembled people heeded Alitherses' words, but there were still a number who sided with Antinous' father and seized their weapons.

Led by Eupeithes, they set off to find Odysseus. Word had got out he had gone up to Laertes' farm, and that is where they made for.

The group inside Laertes' cabin had now finished their meal, and Odysseus told one of them to step outside and look around in case the enemy was coming. One of the sons of Dolius left the table and saw them advancing up the mountainside. He gave Odysseus a warning shout and immediately they all snatched up a weapon and ran outside.

The original four were now reinforced by Dolius' six sons. Their father armed himself as well, and even old

Laertes. For all their years, they were eager to join in the fighting. Heavily outnumbered they may have been but Athena did not leave them to defend themselves unaided, for as the enemy approached she whispered in Laertes' soul:

"Old comrade, make a wish and be the first to hurl your spear."

He raised his withered arm with all the strength left in his aged body, and as he did so power surged into him from the goddess. His throw struck Eupeithes on the cheek-guard of his helmet, tore through the bronze and flung him lifeless to the ground. Odysseus and Telemachus now fell upon the enemy like a raging storm, spreading destruction in their path, while the others followed close behind. Victory was with Odysseus again, and he would have killed them all had he not been restrained by Zeus and Athena herself, who was anxious to save further bloodshed. Zeus hurled a thunderbolt and brought the fighting to an end. Immediately, Athena stepped into their midst in Mentor's form and called a truce. Odysseus, who knew it was the goddess speaking, was glad at heart that the time had come for all of them to live in peace.

THE AUTHOR OF THE ILIAD AND THE ODYSSEY

The Trojan War, which scholars tell us must have taken place around 1200 B.C., marks the end of an epoch. Indeed, within a space of not more than a hundred years, Mycenaean civilization disappeared and a dark age fell on Greece which lasted between two and three centuries. Yet although all else was shrouded in the blanket of the dark, the cultural legacy of the world that had been lost shone through and lived on to become the seed of that brilliant flowering of the Hellenic spirit which was yet to come. What was saved we now call Greek Mythology. Handed down by word of mouth, from one singer to another, around seven hundred years before the birth of Christ it reached the ears of Homer, and from the rich store he had at his disposal he crafted his two immortal epics, the Iliad and the Odyssey. Although these works have come down to us mutilated and 'improved', they still overflow with the inspired words of a giant of poetry, yet one of whom tradition has nothing certain to tell us but his name. But what difference does it make whether Homer was born in Smyrna, on Chios or in Argos, and whether he was blind or not, when we can come to know him through his work, that mirror of his soul?

Homer was a genius whom critics past and present alike have placed at the very summit of the pyramid, alone or accompanied by two or three great names from world literature at most. It is not sufficient for a work of literature to move us by its poetic qualities alone. It must move us, too, by the truth with which it reflects our human condition. Homer excels in both. The poetry of his language often rises to heights of incomparable beauty, as in the parting of Hector from Andromache, or the scene at the end of the 'Iliad' in which Priam asks Achilles for the body of his son. What universal human values are enshrined in this parting! And how can Achilles, who, by dragging Hector's body in the dust, has outraged even the gods who love him, now receive king Priam in his tent? How could he find room for so much sympathy in a heart so filled with bitter rage? Can a man at times be hard and savage and at others kind and yielding? The truth is that he can. This is what our poet told us three thousand years ago, and he is right. But that is Homer for you: measured, decent and above all unbiassed. While he proclaims that 'there is nothing sweeter in the world than mother-land and parents', his vision of humanity is so universal as to have an Achaean and a

Trojan embrace in death. Not for him the good on one side and the evil on the other, but only men ranged in battle against their fellow men. Homer loves his country, but he also loves mankind beyond all national boundaries, and there is no contradiction in this. He loves his homeland and his people best who has the deepest springs of love in him. Many men have been great but not all have been true of heart. Homer was both.